Supporting the Integration of Refugees with Little Formal Education:
An Intercultural Approach

Coordination

Marcelline Bengaly

Writing Committee

Julie Morissette, *Career Counsellor, Ph.D. Candidate in Education,*
Université de Sherbrooke

Annie Gourde, *Career Counsellor, Ph.D. Candidate in Guidance Counselling,*
Université Laval

Liette Goyer, *Career Counsellor, Ph.D., Full Professor,*
Université Laval

Patricia Dionne, *Career Counsellor, Ph.D., Associate Professor,*
Université de Sherbrooke

Marcelline Bengaly, *Ph.D., Full Professor,*
Université Laval

Supporting the Integration of Refugees with Little Formal Education: An Intercultural Approach
Copyright © Julie Morissette, career counsellor, M.A., Annie Gourde, career counsellor, M.A., Liette Goyer, career counsellor, Ph.D., Patricia Dionne, career counsellor, Ph.D., Marcelline Bengaly, Ph.D. (2024)

Published by:
CERIC
Foundation House
Suite 300, 2 St. Clair Avenue East
Toronto, ON
M4T 2T5
Website: www.ceric.ca
Email: admin@ceric.ca

ISBN
Print book: ISBN: 978-1-988066-82-0
eBook ISBN: 978-1-988066-83-7
ePDF: ISBN: 978-1-988066-84-4

Design and layout: Lindsay Maclachlan, Manuela Gaviria
Cover illustration: Ivana Elverdin

Acknowledgments

We gratefully acknowledge the team at the partner organization for their valuable collaboration and contribution to the work leading up to this guide.

To the leadership of the partner organization for their openness and support.

To all the refugees who generously accepted to meet us for interviews.

To CERIC for funding this project.

To the following individuals who graciously accepted to review this guide:

- Joannie Laberge, Career Counsellor
- Yolaine Carver, Career Counsellor
- Lynne Rochon, Coordinator and Immigrant Outreach Worker
- Josée Lapointe, Teacher, Social and Occupational Integration
- Julie Gallant, Teacher, Social and Occupational Integration
- Pascale Corbeil, Teacher, Social and Occupational Integration

Table of Contents

List of Tables

1. Foreword

Supporting immigrants—particularly refugees—in their career guidance and social and occupational integration is not only a professional commitment, but an ethical and political one as well. These newcomers need assistance with developing a plan for integrating into the host society and the labour market that reflects their values and needs and lays the groundwork for a decent life in their new host country. Counsellors need to be able to mediate while respecting intercultural differences and carry out actions to shape environmental conditions that can build bridges or favourable mechanisms—especially with employers and public institutions—so these dreams can be realized. Such an approach presents implications of ethics and equity and demands rethinking the importance that support professionals place on the social and occupational autonomy of refugees. In fact, two kinds of issues appear to be at stake for these professionals. These are related to:

- Social advocacy, in breaking down external or institutional barriers affecting the well-being of the people they serve;
- Professional advocacy, in the face of these barriers that affect the offering of quality professional services to these beneficiaries (Supeno et al., 2023).

This presupposes, as Michaud et al. (2012) point out, walking in solidarity with refugees to facilitate their sustainable integration into the host society. By striving to develop their empowerment (Le Bossé, 2016) and leveraging advocacy strategies (Supeno et al., 2020), actions can be taken with and on behalf of these refugees. Advocacy is considered a relevant resource for vulnerable people who are subject to social inequalities (Arthur, 2014; Arthur & Collins, 2014).

Our intentions for this guide are not simply to enhance understanding of the difficulties in this support work, but also to promote greater justice and respect for certain cultural principles to strengthen the "enabling" character (Robertson & Picard, 2021) of existing policies. The stakes are even higher for refugees with little formal education, who live in rather complex circumstances: after being forcibly displaced, they must now cope with enormous social, cultural and health struggles, compounded by the issue of education. For those dedicated to assisting them, this means immersing oneself in their world, culture (before the displacement), tragedy, migrant story and the agonizing reality of living in refugee camps. Watching documentaries on life in these camps, for example, is a good place to start.[1] It is also essential that all support staff working with refugees—one-on-one or in groups—undertake a substantive self-reflection on their own cultural biases (conscious and unconscious). Only then will it be possible to focus on co-building meaning and effective respect for refugees' cultures, values and the potential they bring with them.

---

1 For videos and articles documenting the deplorable living conditions in refugee camps and hurdles migrants encounter during displacement, see: https://www.doctorswithoutborders.ca/refugees-idps-and-people-on-the-move/?_gl=1*1m2nfgl*_gcl_au*MTAxOTM5NTM5MC4xNzEwMTY3MTM2.

Who is This Guide For?

This guide is intended for anyone whose work involves supporting immigrant refugees—specifically those with little formal education—so they can take their place in the host society and the workplace. It was designed especially with career advisors and guidance counsellors[2] in mind, primarily those working in Adult Education Centres (AECs) or employment assistance organizations. Faculty, teachers and anyone enrolled in various programs in the helping professions will also undoubtedly benefit from the theoretical and practical contributions found herein.

---

2   For the purpose of this guide, the term "counsellor" will be used throughout when referring to these professionals.

Introduction

Background to the Guide

This guide deals with the support provided to refugees with little formal education in their social and occupational integration (SOI). Although some of its content is equally applicable to other immigrant groups with similar educational backgrounds, its central tenet remains the specific and complex predicament of refugees with little formal education. A deeper analysis of these circumstances requires first putting immigration into context.

Some studies reveal that in proportion to the size of its population, "Canada receives more immigrants than any other country in the world" (May, 2022, p.198, free translation). 2021 Census Data (Statistics Canada, 2021)[3] show that 1,328,240 immigrants arrived in Canada between 2016 and 2021—16.3% of them as refugees. [4] The province of Québec received a similar percentage between 1982 and 2017: "16% of all admitted immigrants combined" (Fleury & Luc, 2022, p.43, free translation).

To adapt and settle in their host society, immigrants in general and refugees in particular need to learn a good deal of new things, including the culture, the inner workings of education systems and the labour market, and—above all—language, which is often a priority and a considerable barrier at the same time. Between 2014 and 2018, for instance, 41% of refugees who arrived in the province of Quebec spoke neither French nor English.

Lower levels of formal education—and, in some cases, no schooling at all—can complicate learning and adapting to the host country, especially in a society where reading and writing are an essential part of daily life. With this mind, Francization and literacy programs [5]—funded by the Ministère de l'Éducation in Québec—are very important and play a critical role in the SOI of a sizable number of refugees. The Conseil supérieur de l'éducation (2021) estimates that 10% of those aged 15 and older "has between 0 and 6 years of schooling" (p.20, free translation). These Francization programs are generally offered to newcomers in Adult Education Centres (AECs) and are grounded in a pedagogical approach that fosters social and cultural integration. Refugees with little formal education who take part in these programs are also provided with career guidance and social and occupational integration support, both one-on-one and in groups.

---

3   https://www12.statcan.gc.ca/census-recensement/2021/as-sa/fogs-spg/page cfm?topic=9&Lang=E&dguid=2021A000011124, consulted January 13, 2023

4   60.5% were economic immigrants, 20.2% were sponsored by family and 2.9% emigrated for other reasons.

5   For example, see: https://cdeacf.ca/dossier/alpha-francisation

The Research Project Behind the Guide

This guide is the result of a research project undertaken between 2019 and 2022 aimed at improving career guidance services provided to immigrants. During this CERIC-funded study, the research team, led by CRIEVAT researcher Dr. Marcelline Bengaly, was approached with questions specifically regarding refugees with little formal education.

The challenges of delivering support to refugees with little formal education lie in the complex nature of their migrant experience. In Canada, refugee status is granted (following specific procedures) to people "who are forced to leave their home countries because of serious human rights abuses" (CCR, 2023).[6] This status gives them the right to receive certain services including those that can foster their SOI. However, staff tasked with providing career guidance support to these refugees often find themselves at a loss, since most of the extant research in this field was conducted with qualified immigrants. The same applies to scientific and professional literature, as very few studies have documented the difficulties encountered by refugees with little formal education. In view of this, it is reasonable to assume the existence of a blind spot in the training of career counsellors. How are helping professionals prepared to handle specific challenges in supporting such clients, both individually and in groups?

The research team's approach to this issue began with an in-depth needs analysis. The team held interviews and working sessions with guidance professionals at the Centre Louis-Jolliet. The guidance professionals reflected on the issues they regularly face in the course of their practice. Based on the most acute points in the summary document produced by these professionals, a team of experts was assembled to prepare this guide in the hope of offering answers to the questions raised and to the need of adapting some practices. Indeed, we felt it was particularly important to provide a tool that would help professionals support refugees with little formal education to expand consideration of specific issues of their situation as well as the underlying challenges.

To do so, the research team settled on an overarching objective to:

- Gain a more granular understanding of the components of guidance and counselling for immigrant refugees with little formal education in their career guidance and social and occupational integration, and suggest some approaches for reflection and action.

This overarching objective was broken down into three goals:

1. Present a broad picture of the challenges facing refugees with little formal education in their social and occupational integration (SOI).
2. Provide an intercultural approach to guidance and counselling for these refugees in their career guidance and SOI.
3. Propose an intercultural guidance process to support this approach.

---

6   To learn more, see: https://ccrweb.ca/en/information-refugees

This guide is structured around these three goals. Part One is devoted to the different challenges faced by refugees with little formal education, with suggested intervention approaches for specific challenges. Adopting these approaches will be made easier by reading Part Two, where theoretical models related to the concepts of cultural differences are discussed at length. Part Three proposes intercultural intervention approaches that consider these models and Part Four describes in detail the guidance process that forms the backbone of this approach.

Part One

Understanding and Responding to the Specific Challenges of Refugees with Little Formal Education

Seven Key Challenges Faced by Refugees with Little Formal Education

The number one concern for most immigrants lies in stabilizing their living conditions in the host country: financial situation, professional life, language, health, work/family balance, housing, social relationships, access to government services, and so on. For refugees with little formal education, settling into a new life is even more daunting: not only do they encounter the same challenges as other immigrants, but some also likely experience distinctive struggles resulting from the singular nature of their migration experience, a journey often marked by armed conflicts, insecurity and violence (Joly, 2019; Richard & Bombardier, 2020; UNHCR, 2023). Low levels of education (or in some cases no formal education at all) also compound the complexity of each of these challenges.

These distinctive challenges were repeatedly stressed by education centre staff members working with refugees (CSE, 2021). In fact, "customized approaches" had to be used because of the complex and multi-factorial nature of the struggles this population had to contend with:

> Trauma-induced mental health problems, family obligations, lone parenthood, difficulty in adapting to Québec, learning and/or behavioural disorders or challenges, poor health, etc. For some of them, moreover, learning only really begins after several months of adaptation (p.82, free translation).

Based on these multiple challenges, some key characteristics of the unique situation of refugees with little formal education are presented below, grouped under seven major themes:

1. Education and language skills development;
2. Communicating and understanding information;
3. Physical and mental health;
4. Precarity and a sense of urgent need;
5. Learning the social codes of the host society;
6. Employment readiness and the labour market;
7. Knowledge of and access to government and community resources.

For each of these themes, we will expound on the challenges refugees with little formal education are likely to encounter. To better equip counsellors who work with these clients, this will be followed by suggested intervention approaches and collaborative and environmental resources drawn from scientific literature.

1
Education and Language Skills Development

1.1   Main Challenges

* *Learning the Basics of Reading and Writing in a New Language*

A large percentage of refugees does not possess a working knowledge of reading and writing, even in their mother tongue, which Dubé (2014) and Seufert (1999) note can make it challenging to learn a new language. Arsenault (2021) concurs by highlighting how a low level of literacy among these refugees can significantly increase "the difficulties of acquiring a spoken language, which in turn affect job integration, access to healthcare and developing social connections with the mainstream population of the host society" (p.5, free translation). Additionally, this learning process occurs in an education system run by rules that refugees are wholly unfamiliar with. They can therefore run into difficulties understanding requirements and responsibilities, which they may then struggle to fulfil (Bimrose & McNair, 2011; Gibbons et al., 2019; Seufert, 1999). Consequently, teachers often have to be inventive and adapt their teaching methods (Seufert, 1999).

For many allophones whose mother tongue is far removed from French (e.g., Persian, Hindi and Cambodian, which do not share the same alphabet or phonological similarities), learning the language can also be a major hurdle. For refugees with little formal education from some corners of the world, the difficulty of learning French is heightened by their low literacy skills and other challenges related to their migration experience (Laberge, 2020).

Additionally, the Québécois French spoken in Québec does not always match the more standard variety taught in classrooms or used in other French-speaking countries (CSE, 2021). This can lead to communication breakdowns in the workplace and in daily activities. These difficulties in learning French can leave some people "feeling shy or afraid" (Dubé, 2014, p. 79, free translation) and, most of all, lacking self-confidence.

* *Communicating and Integrating into the Host Society*

While learning a new language, refugees with little formal education also have to take steps to integrate into society and the workplace: fulfilling administrative formalities, booking and travelling to appointments, juggling priorities, etc. These actions require not only the need for written and spoken French language skills, but also many new points of reference to help them navigate the host society. On top of this is the fact that some refugees may find it difficult to articulate their own needs, unlike what is generally expected in Québec. Among those from communitarian societies, for example, making choices tends to revolve around community or family needs; having to take a position and share personal needs can be a tall order for them. All these factors combined can slow their pace of learning and performance of some tasks—hence the importance of providing tailored support to develop refugees' ability to more easily manage their daily lives in the host society.

- *Balancing Family and School*

For refugees with little formal education, the lack of resources to facilitate balancing family, work and language skills development acts as a disincentive to learning French (Prévost, 2021). Many find it difficult to reconcile heavy family responsibilities (e.g., finding childcare, health issues) with the demands of taking French courses (CSE, 2021; Seufert, 1999). They often lack time and or energy or may not be emotionally ready for different reasons (e.g., anxiety, depression, lack of motivation).

- *Overcoming Personal Limitations for Learning*

The Conseil supérieur de l'éducation (2021) has noted several factors that affect refugee learning in the host society; age, for example, can affect self-awareness and learning ability. Refugees with little formal education may also be living with one or more disabilities or learning difficulties or disorders:

> Learning readiness can also depend on the state of mind of the potential learner; stress, mental or physical health, cultural shock or post-traumatic stress disorder are also all intrinsic barriers to fully engaging in learning a new language (ibid., p.77, free translation).

Ultimately, learning a language and regularly attending French class cannot be pinned down to a simple matter of "motivation."

1.2   Suggested Intervention Approaches and Resources

The summary in the table below is derived from an analysis of 1) key research (e.g., CSE, 2021; Prévost, 2021; RQuODE, 2016; Udayar et al., 2020), and 2) first-hand experiences of staff working to support refugees with little formal education. The first column lists the most common challenges often encountered by these refugees. In the second column are suggested intervention approaches for counsellors to support this group, accompanied in the third column by possible collaborative and/or environmental resources.

Table 1. Education and Language Skills: Summary of Intervention Challenges, Approaches and Resources

Education and Language Skills		
Challenge	**Approaches for Counsellors**	**Resources**
Learning the basics of reading and writing in a new language	• Seize opportunities during interventions to explain to refugees the importance of practising reading French (e.g., signs, cereal boxes) and speaking French in different settings. • Encourage writing in French (e.g., grocery lists, greetings, a note in their children's lunchbox) at every opportunity. • Propose getting involved in community activities. • Encourage them not to be too hard on themselves about not having time or making mistakes. • Inspire them to persevere in their learning. • Given that refugees might avoid talking as a form of protection, verify if this is the case and then talk with them about what they need to feel safe. • Create an environment where they can regularly practise their French. • Recommend watching French TV programs and/or web series (particularly Québecois ones) and listening to French radio and/or podcasts. • Promote oral activities to continue learning French. As for writing, use simple, illustrated and practical material when exploring different labour sectors. • Opt for authentic material (e.g., real bus schedules, radio programs, restaurant menus, job applications).	• Francization courses • Immigrant and refugee assistance centres • Services Québec • Service Canada • United for Literacy / Littératie ensemble • Community organizations • Social networks (counsellor's and refugee's) • Teachers and support workers

Education and Language Skills: Summary of Intervention Challenges, Approaches and Resources

Education and Language Skills		
Challenge	**Approaches for Counsellors**	**Resources**
Communicating and integrating into the host society	• Use hands-on activities such as photography or scrapbooking to help refugees identify what is important for them, their needs and those of their community, and challenges encountered in the host society (Rey et al., 2019). • Support them through the steps needed to integrate into the host society and refer them if they need more help. • Invite refugees who have successfully integrated to share their stories (storytelling). • Call on volunteers to talk about challenges they faced during their integration or ask the group to share critical incidents and, where possible, explore solutions together. • Create links between cultural codes learnings in the Francization program.	• Francization groups • Community organizations • Intercultural community workers and volunteers • Refugees who have successfully integrated • Cellphones for taking pictures • Storytelling resources (Oral History Association, 2009; Shanouda & Yoshida, 2012).
Balancing family and school	• Encourage refugees to speak French at home by setting a time for the family to practise together (e.g., between 6:00 and 7:00 in the evening and for half a day on the weekend). • Discuss organizational strategies and task sharing as a couple.	• Children, spouse/life partner • Family and friends • Community organizations
Overcoming personal limitations for learning	• Encourage refugees to stop feeling powerless by pointing out positive things that can be done (provided these are meaningful to them). • Listen to their fears and help them through their grief.	• Literacy and Francization teaching staff • Support workers • Community organizations

2
Communicating and Understanding Information

2.1   Main Challenges

- *Integrating into a Society Without Understanding its Language Codes*

Operating in and navigating a new environment without fully understanding its language codes can be tremendously challenging in terms of communicating and accessing information (Roesti, 2019). Having difficulty communicating, reading or writing can make refugees with little formal education particularly vulnerable in many instances:

> [...] whether it is with their children's teachers, landlords, shopkeepers, governmental and administrative bodies or having to go to a hospital emergency room. Additionally, the time it takes to become literate and proficient in French can vary and sometimes the pace can be quite slow (Arsenault, 2020, p. 25, free translation).

These challenges can also affect refugees' relationships with others. People who are unable to adequately communicate can sometimes become impatient or irritated when they do not understand, both in formal and informal settings, such as "talking to the owner of the building where they live, calling Hydro-Québec or Bell, talking on the phone or to Quebeckers" (Dubé, 2014, p. 75, free translation). The fact of not understanding is a major stumbling block in the many spheres of a refugee's life.

- *Accessing Information in an Increasingly Digital World*

La communication, qu'elle soit en personne ou au moyen des technologies de l'information et des communications (TIC), représente un défi important pour les personnes réfugiées faiblement scolarisées (Robert, 2021). Que ce soit pour obtenir des informations sur le monde scolaire ou sur le marché du travail (IMT), trouver un logement, effectuer différentes démarches auprès des instances gouvernementales, ou même pour apprendre la langue, ces moyens sont désormais incontournables. Chaque situation du quotidien devient ainsi un combat pour ces personnes, ce qui contribue à complexifier leur expérience (Beaulieu, 2019). Le fait de ne pas savoir utiliser un ordinateur ou naviguer sur Internet peut réduire considérablement leur « espace des possibles » (Sen, 2010). De plus, vivant dans des conditions financières précaires, ces personnes ne sont pas toujours en mesure de s'offrir des services d'accès à Internet. Elles deviennent alors dépendantes de ceux offerts gratuitement, mais pas n'importe quand, dans certains lieux publics (Robert, 2021).

2.2   Suggested Intervention Approaches and Resources

The table below is based both on an analysis of experiences of people who work on the ground with the refugee population and recommendations and suggestions derived from research (CSE, 2021; Dionne et al., 2022a; RQuODE, 2016).

Table 2. Communicating and Understanding Information: Summary of Intervention Challenges, Approaches and Resources

Communicating and Understanding Information		
Challenge	**Approaches for Counsellors**	**Resources**
Integrating into a society without understanding its	• Ask refugees open-ended questions to help expand on specific vocabulary associated with the topic at hand and regularly ask them to rephrase to ensure they understand the information. • Rephrase what you say. This does not mean repeating ad nauseum nor talking loudly: they heard, but they may not understand. • Propose a variety of activities when exploring the job market, trades and professions. • Organize an activity on naming jobs featured in a film. • Organize theme or regional career exploration days. • Organize tours and/or internships with local companies. • Explain dos and don'ts in verbal (written and spoken) and non-verbal communication to ensure refugees understand the often-unspoken meaning of cultural expectations (e.g., how to get in touch with someone, standard polite forms of address, how to leave a phone message). • Conduct mock interviews asking typical job interview questions.	• Memory games about occupations • Videos about trades and professions • Local businesses • Employment counsellors • Services Québec • Service Canada

Communicating and Understanding Information: Summary of Intervention Challenges, Approaches and Resources

Communicating and Understanding Information		
Challenge	**Approaches for Counsellors**	**Resources**
Accessing information in an increasingly digital world	• Plan computer workshops to introduce refugees to basic digital literacy (e.g., email, Internet, online job searches, GPS applications such as Google Maps, voicemail). • Encourage a broad range of learning opportunities by using smartphones. Feel free to use devices during career exploration and career guidance activities. • Introduce text-to-speech and immersive reader apps to help with comprehension and improve pronunciation. • Provide continuous support for career exploration, training and employment.	• Basic computer skills courses at some community organizations • Immersive reader apps • Employment counsellors • Employment assistance organizations • Francization teachers • Services Québec

3
Physical and Mental Health

3.1   Main Challenges

Prior to their arrival in Canada, many refugees suffered trauma, either related to events at the root of their forced departure or during their migration. Indeed, they are often victims of or witnesses to a least one horrific event, if not many: torture, violence, genocide, physical and/or sexual assault, natural disasters, war, execution or murder of family member(s), family dislocation, etc. It is crucial, therefore, that those who work to support them in their social and occupational integration (SOI) have at least a basic understanding of these traumas and their impact on the integration process.

Trauma is a physiological, emotional and cognitive response to a major stressful situation or repeated exposure to stress over a long period of time. According to the American Psychological Association (APA, 2022):

> Trauma is an emotional response to a terrible event like an accident, rape, or natural disaster. Immediately after the event, shock and denial are typical. Longer term reactions include unpredictable emotions, flashbacks, strained relationships, and even physical symptoms like headaches or nausea (paragraph 1 APA, n.d.).[7]

Although this emotional response is altogether normal in light of a traumatic event, it can also significantly alter the functioning of an individual, causing overwhelming distress likely to impact the integration of a refugee with little formal education. Trauma can induce two major pathological conditions: Post Traumatic Stress Disorder (PTSD) and Complex Post Traumatic Stress Disorder (CPTSD). The main difference between the two lies in their recurrence: PTSD is typically the result of a single major traumatic incident, while the second stems from a succession of events or repeated trauma of a certain duration. These two conditions can cause dysfunction because they affect the body's ability to adapt (Albaret, 2020). CPTSD can also trigger changes in emotion, identity and interpersonal relationships (Krammer et al., 2016; Van Dijke et al., 2018) brought on by an overload of the response system to stress. This sets off a "series of hormonal alterations that organize the brain to deal with a hostile situation" (Wilkinson, 2003, p.237, free translation). Excessive (too much or too little) or inadequate reactions can then occur (Collin-Vézina, 2016).

Comparative studies of the general population show that victims of PTSD or CPTSD (which afflicts many refugees) can also be seen in shortfalls in their cognitive and language processes (ibid., 2016). They appear

---

7   https://www.apa.org/topics/trauma#:~:text=Trauma%20is%20an%20emotional%20response,symptoms%20 like%20headaches%20or%20nausea, consulted August 22, 2023

to have more difficulty related to working memory, inhibitory control,[8] cognitive flexibility, planning and problem solving. They can, for example, exhibit problems related to attention, language, an altered ability to process information, anticipating the consequences of their actions, sleep problems, amplified personality traits, lower pain tolerance, heightened anxiety (panic attacks, excessive fear), difficulty in controlling emotions (anger, impulsiveness), hypersensitivity to environmental stimuli (noise, light), emotional neutrality, emotional indifference (lack of empathy), depression, irritability (nervousness), withdrawal, sense of hopelessness (loss of life meaning), and difficulty imagining a future self (Frounfelker et al., 2021; Salhi et al., 2020; Scoglio & Salhi, 2021).

As for their identity sense, trauma victims ultimately may have difficulties in relating to others and the environment they inhabit (Kirmayer, 2002). These can be symptoms of the self-image of a person "under constant threat" and, as a result, trauma victims may develop additional defence mechanisms to cope with the outside world. Individuals who are always looking outward and toward others to protect themselves may be especially vulnerable to other people and external demands, and may also create an inner void (Bigras et al., 2015; Rousseau, 2000). This often leads to confusion, low self-esteem, and a lack of confidence, perception and judgment.

The potential presence of dissociative symptoms can alter identity and self-representation (Van der Kolk, 2015), exhibited in, for example:

- A sense of disconnection from the self, detachment from part of the self or like living "on autopilot";
- Confusing thoughts and feelings;
- Self-estrangement;
- Estrangement from one's environment;
- Feeling detached from time or that time no longer passes in the same way.

Similarly, memory loss, as well as forgetfulness or poor recollection of facts and events, can greatly inhibit some refugees from speaking up or asking for help. For others, they have trouble telling their story or are uncomfortable with the idea of not being able to answer certain questions (Van der Kolk, 2015).

- *Rebuilding the Self in Response to Complex Transitions*

The intricate transition experienced by refugees should ideally be examined through the lens of their trauma, paths and challenges of adapting to a new environment. To help them navigate this process, it is crucial we know how to analyze the course of the transition, if we are to understand the phenomena at play (Schlossberg et al., 1995; Schlossberg, 2005). In reality, this is not a single transition but rather three: ecological, psychosocial and unanticipated.

Bronfenbrenner (1976, 1979, 2004) defines an ecological transition as one where a change in setting forces the individual into a process of shuffling identities to strike the right "mutual adjustment" between two settings—the one the individual leaves behind and the one into which they integrate. They have to revisit

---

8   Inhibitory control is a cognitive process that enables resisting the temptation for motor response or intuitive strategies and selecting information that is only relevant to performing a task (Houdé, 2014).

their entire value system, create a new list of roles, new models of action and restructure their self-representation to bridge these two settings. For refugees, such changes are major disruptors that can manifest through a certain disconnect—the feeling of being a stranger in their environment, for example.

A transition from a *psychosocial* perspective is much more complex than a simple passage from one setting to another. In fact, the situation refugees find themselves in represents a major upheaval in their lives. The way they represent their existence[9] following one or more events is that their "life space" [10] is flipped upside down, compelling them to "rearrange their worldviews" (Guichard & Huteau, 2007, p.432, inspired by Parkes, 1971, 1975, free translation).

All transitions can be stressful. Those that refugees with little formal education experience can also be examined through the lens of stress and adaptation strategies, using the Schlossberg approach (inspired by Lazarus and Folkman, 1984), which defines transition as "any event or non-event that notably affects the daily life of an individual: changing relationships, routines, beliefs, roles" (Schlossberg, cited in Guichard and Huteau 2005, p.50, free translation). Of the three types of transitions Schlossberg identifies, "unanticipated transitions" are particularly germane to keep in mind in supporting refugees.[11]

In the case of a refugee faced with complex transitions, internal and external changes occur and create imbalances. Managing this situation entails inventing new terms of reference, which in turn means rebuilding the self and redefining the meaning of the choices made. However, this process does not unfold the same way for everyone: transitions that are seemingly alike can generate different responses (Anderson et al., 2012). These inter-individual differences can be explained by enablers or inhibitors related to situation, self, support and strategies, known as the 4S System.[12]

• *Overcoming Learning Challenges in Complex Transitions*

Because of the various traumas associated with refugees' intricate transitions, integrating into a new host society involves absorbing vast amounts of new knowledge, as well as great cultural adaptability in carrying out rebuilding the self and searching for the meaning of the transitional situation (Olry-Louis, 2020). As discussed above, the different forms of refugee traumas can affect memory, attention span, concentration and the ability to process information. It can also lead to language and problem-solving difficulties, as well as affect the ability to imagine a future self (Olry-Louis, 2020).

The issues described above are common across refugee populations and contribute to making them less receptive to learning (Arsenault, 2020). Moreover, refugees with little formal education are in a

---

9   This refers to the way individuals represent their existence, knowledge and beliefs: "interpretations of the past, expectations for the future, plans and biases. These representations include not only a model of the world as perceived by the individual, but also probable, ideal and feared models" (Guichard & Huteau, 2007, p. 432, free translation).

10   "Life space" refers to all the phenomena that play a role in the life of an individual. It includes everything that determines behaviours (e.g., memories, the environment inhabited, interactions with others, perception of this environment and the world). It is "all the events likely to determine a person's behaviour: everything we should know to account for their behaviour in a given context and at a given time" (Guichard & Huteau, 2005, p. 48, free translation).

11   The other two types of transitions are 1) anticipated transitions, or foreseen or planned events, and 2) non-event transitions, or expected events that did not happen.

12   For more on the 4S system refer to Anderson et al. (2012).

particularly tricky spot as they not only have to absorb new cultural norms, but also a learning system that hinges on using cognitive and affective resources that might have been compromised by their complex transitional experiences. Low literacy and language barriers can also make this population more vulnerable to social isolation and, as a result, worsen their already weakened mental health. The "Life space" refers to all the phenomena that play a role in the life of an individual. It includes everything that determines behaviours (e.g., memories, the environment inhabited, interactions with others, perception of this environment and the world). It is "all the events likely to determine a person's behaviour: everything we should know to account for their behaviour in a given context and at a given time" (Guichard & Huteau, 2005, p. 48, free translation). cumulative effect of these factors can put the brakes on their integration.

3.2 Suggested Intervention Approaches and Resources

To be able to adopt a caring, understanding and non-judgmental approach in supporting refugees, it appears critical to first and foremost keep the impact of traumas and their manifestation on physical and mental health top of mind. As Kirmayer (2002) notes: "the trauma experience can alter self-narratives" (p.743, free translation). In such cases, what might be construed as denial or as "a lie" is in essence a process of self-rebuilding.

Supporting refugees thus entails paying particular attention to the story they tell and being mindful when analyzing it to properly grasp its role and importance. In fact, storytelling is one strategy used to build a new identity and strike a degree of cognitive balance, whether it occurs in an internal monologue, in private conversations, or as part of public representations (Kirmayer, 2002). It can also help to steer cognition, reframe the experience and create an autobiographical self while being conscious of personal and historical continuity.

In their research work on support practices in SOI groups, Dionne et al. (2022a) also suggest creating a space for legitimate exchange that lets refugees reconnect to their subjective experience in refugee camps. The resulting mental and emotional awareness helps them find a different meaning in this experience: they might, for example, be able to recognize their courage, strengths and resilience. As in Section 2, the table below includes approaches drawn from an analysis of experiences of support workers assisting this target population and several pertinent studies (e.g., Association canadienne pour la santé mentale, 2003; El-Awad et al., 2022; Grochtdreis et al., 2022; Lambert, 2014; Lin et al., 2020; Vonnahme et al., 2015).

Table 3. Physical and Mental Health: Summary of Intervention Challenges, Approaches and Resources

Physical and Mental Health		
Challenge	**Approaches for Counsellors**	**Resources**
Coping with the effects of trauma	• Encourage refugees to participate in group discussions, coffee club meetings and family activities. • Refer them to sharing groups to help them open up about their struggles and share coping strategies. • Demystify stress and its symptoms. • During discussions, help them identify strengths they developed that might give this hard experience some meaning.	• Family and friends • Places of worship or religious communities • Local community services centres (CLSCs) and hospitals • Professional mental health and human relations resources • Centre for Studies on Human Stress / Centre d'études sur le stress humain **website** and resources • Community organizations • Discussion groups
Overcoming learning difficulties associated with physical or mental health issues	• Refer refugees to and assist them to effectively use resources. • Support school success and perseverance. • Where possible, get involved in their network to raise awareness about the need for encouragement and support.	• Other education support professionals (e.g., resource teachers, educators, psychologists, social workers) • Family and friends
Rebuilding the self in response to complex transitions	• Assist refugees in getting help based on their needs. • Support them in getting out of social isolation. • Where appropriate, encourage religious practice and help them find places of worship. • Assist them in learning about online resources. • Create a list of local resources. • Help them find a job to get them out of social isolation and meet people. • Work on building identity as part of the guidance process.	• Family and friends • Religious communities • Employment assistance organizations • Community organizations • Placement agencies • Employment counsellors • Info-Social 811 • Local social service programs on the 211 Québec website • UNHCR (United Nations High Commissioner for Refugees) Canada's website • Gouvernement du Québec's Getting Better... My Way website

4
Precarity and a Sense of Urgent Need

4.1 Main Challenges

- *A Family to Support, an Immediate Need to Work*

Many refugees have spent a large part of their lives either in a constant state of emergency or in survival mode. This can affect steps taken to integrate into the job market and their experiences during the learning period required for this integration. The duration of allowances and level of financial support for mandatory, government-provided training is limited and often inadequate, which also heightens the desire among some refugees to want to find a job as quickly as possible.

For refugees with little formal education, financial uncertainty is a major source of anxiety over being able to provide for family and pay for day-to-day expenses such as food, rent or daycare. The inability to cover basic living needs for themselves and/or for their family can not only affect their health, but also delay various steps that could help them with their SOI (Lavoie et al., 2008; Vonnahme et al., 2015). In fact, because of a lack of time and means, they may not be able to fully engage in the career guidance process. The urgent need to swiftly find a job and be the family's breadwinner is certainly a priority, but equally important is the fact that this precarity could also impinge on their ability to see themselves in a medium— to long-term plan that could bring a different contribution to their community and by extension to the host society in general.

- *Gaining a Foothold in the Host Society*

Getting a job can help refugees climb out of precarity and integrate socially. For this reason, refugees have the "resolve to gain a foothold in the host society, both for themselves and [for] their families" (CSE, 2021, p.11, free translation). However, this realignment can often produce a certain ambivalence between "living better and the challenges in understanding how the new environment works" (Roesti, 2019, p.51, free translation). While refugees may no longer feel in danger (as they did in their country of origin), they have to cope with many day-to-day challenges in adapting to their new environment: understanding new ways of living, values, traditions, eating habits, daily chores and so on. Access to public transit and very long commutes to get to work or to a training centre[13] can also create additional strain (Arsenault, 2020). In Québec, adapting to the weather is no small matter either: winter drives some refugees to further isolate, which inevitably means fewer social interactions.

---

13 In cities, more affordable housing tends to be located on the outskirts, which are often less well served by public transit.

- *Finding Decent and Affordable Housing*

For refugee families, finding a decent place to live can prove to be a near-insurmountable obstacle due to current housing shortages, the cost of rent or refusal by some landlords to let to prospective racialized renters (Arsenault, 2020; Guay-Charrette, 2010). And when they do find a place, let us not forget that refugees will need to familiarize themselves with how renting (e.g., signing a lease, paying rent, contacting the landlord), utilities and sanitation services work (Arsenault, 2020).

4.2   Suggested Intervention Approaches and Resources

In general, it is important to know about the financial situation of refugees and to continually work together with various services to facilitate access to assistance resources. It is also appropriate to continue with the career guidance process even after they find employment.

Dionne et al. (2022b) also show the benefits of intervention based on agency – that is, the ability to make choices and shape one's life course. This approach may help refugees with little formal education realize that learning can happen through interaction with others, by being familiar with societal norms, and by using their own agency and ability to understand aspects of the culture from a perspective they value.

The summary of challenges, approaches and resources for interventions in the table that follows is once again based on an analysis of the experiences of professionals who work with the target population and a review of literature (Arsenault, 2020; Beaulieu, 2019; CSE, 2021; Guay-Charrette, 2010; Sue & Sue, 2015; Zalaquett & Chambers, 2017).

Table 4. Precarity and a Sense of Urgent Need: Summary of Intervention Challenges, Approaches and Resources

Precarity and a Sense of Urgent Need		
Challenge	**Approaches for Counsellors**	**Resources**
A family to support, an immediate need to work	• Provide help and answer queries from refugees about steps in settling and integrating (e.g., finding a daycare, filling out forms, understanding a letter from the government, wearing winter clothing to keep warm, preparing easy recipes). • Refer them to people in their social network to help them find community resources. • Inform them about available services. • Convey clear and accurate information about assistance measures and allowances.	• Community organizations • Social networks • Food banks • Thrift stores • Municipal services • Directory of organizations in different municipalities • Neighbourhood social service programs on the 211 Quebec website
Gaining a foothold in the host society	• Refer refugees to support structures in their community to develop their agency. • Help them learn about food products available in the host society by using grocery flyers and encourage them to take part in community cooking workshops on how to prepare it. • Help them understand the job market and its workplace cultural codes. • Help them to find a job, prepare a resume and rehearse job interviews. • Create a sense of belonging; turn adult education centres or organizations into a living space, a trusted environment.	• Staff in Adult Education Centres (AECs) • Employment assistance organizations • Québec Collective Kitchens Association • Community organizations • Basic and adult education institutions • Local community services centre (CLSC) support workers
Finding decent and affordable housing	• Provide information on and refer refugees to financial aid programs. • Provide technical assistance in filling out administrative forms as needed or refer them to a person who can help. • Provide contact information about organizations during an appeal. • Refer them to workshops on housekeeping and using and cleaning appliances.	• Social housing • Co-operative housing • Last-resort financial assistance • Community organizations • Social workers and community workers • Legal aid services such as Juripop

5
Learning the Social Codes of the Host Society

5.1   Main Challenges

- *Learning the Social Codes of the Host Society*

Whether integrating socially or professionally, refugees need to learn and understand the codes of the host society, which may differ from the cultural perspectives, beliefs, values and worldviews of their country of origin (Fouad & Bryars-Winston, 2005). Most refugees who enrol in Francization or literacy courses come primarily from countries where social representations of selfhood differ in many respects from that which is prevalent in Québec. The customary relationship to authority in the home context of the refugee can also be completely different[14] and poor language proficiency may only make things worse. In the workplace, this can be problematic when it comes to interacting with those in positions of authority. On the flip side, management can misinterpret the meaning of a refugee's initiative, ability to learn a task, demonstrate motivation, etc. Another example (although not limited to those with little formal education) is related to legally binding and socially accepted gendered relations in Québec, which contrast sharply with those prevailing in many of refugees' countries of origin. All these examples provide a glimpse into the disorienting culture shock experienced by refugees with little formal education as they seek to fit into their host society.

- *Balancing Family Obligations with the Integration Process*

According to the Conseil supérieur de l'éducation (2021), the integration of some women who arrive as immigrants or refugees can be affected by the social codes of their country of origin, such as the gendered division of household tasks: "stumbling blocks tied to family obligations that can slow down their progress and curtail their learning efforts" (ibid., p.57, free translation). It has been noted, in fact, that women refugees with little formal education are most often the primary caregivers for their children (looking after, supervising and being there for them in times of need) and family (planning and preparing meals, laundry, household chores, etc.). They are also the anchor point of the family, responsible for maintaining ties with the "old country." The time spent on these roles can quickly add up and hold them back from learning French or finding a job, while their spouses can devote more time to this.

---

14 See Table 14 in Part Two.

- *Coping with Adversity*

Discrimination and racism are among the most acute challenges facing refugees—especially those from racialized groups. Thus, even when they manage to learn French, their efforts in the workplace are not always recognized in the same way as those who are native-born (CSE, 2021; Moisan, 2020). Despite current labour shortages, which would seem to make it easier for refugees to enter the workforce, true SOI still requires vigilance today. Lamar et al. (2019) reveal, for example, that racialized women are the ones most at risk because they find themselves faced with overlapping and concurrent forms of racism and discrimination, living in poverty and likely having to cope with added challenges in the education system and in the labour market.

5.2   Suggested Intervention Approaches and Resources

In general, support centred on self-knowledge, personal success and freedom of choice might require targeted consideration in the case of refugees with little formal education. It would be wise to add members of their family and community to assist them in adopting social codes. These aspects will be examined in greater depth below.

In addition to the analysis of the experiences of professionals who work with this population, the summary of challenges, approaches and resources in the table below also takes into account recent literature, such as a paper authored by Arsenault (2020) and a brief by the Conseil supérieur de l'éducation (2021) on the inclusion of immigrant families.

Table 5. Learning the Social Codes of the Host Society: Summary of Intervention Challenges, Approaches and Resources

Learning the Social Codes of the Host Society		
Challenge	**Approaches for Counsellors**	**Resources**
Learning the social codes of the host society	• Encourage intercultural mentoring of families. • Take part in community awareness activities. • Accompany refugees or encourage them to take part in community activities with support workers. • Explain the differences and similarities between the host society culture and other cultures. • Encourage and advise on networking with local players. • Promote host society cultural events to help them integrate. • Support developing interpersonal skills through practical interaction in the living environment (i.e., adult education centre [AEC] or organizations).	• Counsellors • Francization teachers • Company HR personnel • Municipality websites or social media to learn about local activities • Cultural activities • Adult education centres (AECs) • Community organizations • Religious communities • Social networks
Balancing family obligations with the integration process	• Raise awareness of the importance of home visits by support workers. • Provide information about the availability of child drop-in centres and summer camps and refer to the appropriate resources as needed. • Answer questions and help to understand how their children's school works.	• Community organizations such as family resource centres (e.g., Maison de la Famille) providing drop-in childcare • Summer camps • Social workers and community workers • Local community services centres (CLSCs) and the health care network
Coping with adversity	• Promote to businesses the strengths of different cultural communities, as well as their eagerness to integrate in the host society. • Provide workshops in the community to demystify diversity and reduce prejudice. • Ask for local businesses to get involved in the integration of refugees. • Use workshops and electronic means to raise awareness among company HR personnel about cultural differences and their benefits to the company. • Provide a place where refugees can have a voice and be heard about the challenges they encounter.	• Target charities (e.g., food banks) • Multidisciplinary and multicultural teams • Company HR personnel • Services Québec • Service Canada

6
Employment Readiness and the Labour Market

6.1 Main Challenges

- *Knowing How the Labour Market Works*

In light of current labour shortages in Québec, integrating and keeping refugees with little formal education employed in low-skilled jobs may look easy. However, job integration is often a complicated matter that goes beyond merely landing a position and requires considering together with these jobseekers the specifics and conditions of the labour market (Rousseau & Venter, 2009; Roesti, 2019). These can be obstacles for them, and when these refugees do not receive adequate support, they could face:

> [M]isinformation about the job market or the target sector and its requirements [...] lack of networking [...] high standards in French language proficiency [...] systemic barriers to being able to perform at work [...] (problems accessing childcare services or underdeveloped public transit systems) [...] needing a diploma or work experience in Québec [...] forms of discrimination that impact job integration (CSE, 2021, pp.145-148, free translation).

Refugees with little formal education thus need support to familiarize themselves with and grasp not only the specifics of the labour market in Québec, but workplace culture as well. Integrating into the labour market and remaining employed will be easier when they know how to deal with misinformation or administrative formalities in the workplace.

- *Knowing About Employee Rights and Responsibilities*

Anyone integrating into the workplace can be vulnerable when they lack information or are unaware of their rights and responsibilities under the Labour Code or the Act Respecting Occupational Health and Safety (Salamanca, 2016). For refugees with little formal education and low literacy levels, this is all the more true. They could fall prey to exploitation by company HR or employment agencies, when, for example, there is "failure to pay for hours worked, vacation, overtime, breaks and public holidays" (ibid., free translation). Working conditions can also be difficult or unsafe, the pace abusive and "discriminatory practices" such as failure to comply with rules governing meal and break periods may abound (Beaulieu, 2019; Salamanca, 2016). Because of their legal status, fear of losing their job may compel refugees not to defend or assert their rights.

As for employee duties and responsibilities, some refugees with little formal education are likely to have trouble understanding workplace culture in the host country (Dubé, 2014). There can be a mismatch between the specific requirements of the position they hold and what they had known in their previous jobs, such as "arriving on time, not exceeding the number of time off days granted by the company, [or] getting used to taking personal appointments in the evening when getting paid time off is not granted" (ibid., free translation), to name but a few.

- *Remaining Employed*

Refugees are, generally speaking, motivated and show a real desire to do what is required for them to keep their job, even though they might not be familiar with the workplace culture and probably even less so their chosen occupation. Their perception of the labour market in the host country is not representative of the different realities (CSE, 2021) they might have dealt with in their culture of origin. Keeping a job is thus an added challenge and exerts financial pressure on refugees, as they want to ensure they can provide for their family—both here and in their country of origin—and for their children's future. Added to this are the daily challenges of work/family balance, something all too familiar to any native-born employee. Those who depend on public transit may also need to juggle getting children ready in the morning for school or daycare with transit schedules and then try to pick up them up on time to avoid paying extra for extended daycare.

At work, many are not very aware of the skills and aptitudes they have developed to tackle the realities of their host country. They often lack self-confidence, and this can make it difficult for them to see themselves in the role of employee. In some cases, cultural differences may turn out to be the root cause of a misunderstanding, both on their part or the part of the employer or manager. For example, there may be a different understanding of how to communicate with authority, manage a task or what attitudes and behaviours are acceptable or should be avoided with co-workers.[15]

6.2   Suggested Intervention Approaches and Resources

The challenges facing refugees with little formal education in the areas of employment readiness and integration into the labour force can be overcome through support. In a study by Dionne et al. (2022b), for example, following an exercise about things to be proud of and writing a resume, a female participant was better able to recognize her skills and voice her interest in developing them further in the job market. Combined with acquiring relevant knowledge about the labour market, this type of self-recognition skills exercise can help refugees with little formal education be in a better position to envision themselves in the role of employee, one they may not have held for many years because of their migration history.

In other cases, intercultural mediation is what works best. Given that counsellors are familiar with language and social codes, they can more easily approach the employer or daycare manager as an advocate to negotiate an agreement about whatever the issue may be—time schedules, for example. In this way, needs and constraints can be better understood and taken into consideration in relation to the particular work, education or daycare environment (Dionne et al. 2022b).

---

15   We will elaborate on these cultural differences in Part Two.

As in the preceding sections, the following table of challenges, approaches and resources is based on relevant literature (Béji & Pellerin, 2010; Delory-Momberger & Mbiatong, 2011; Dionne et al., 2022b; RQuODE, 2016) and an analysis of the experience of people working with refugees with little formal education.

Table 6. Employment Readiness and the Labour Market: Summary of Intervention Challenges, Approaches and Resources

Employment Readiness and the Labour Market		
Challenge	**Approaches for Counsellors**	**Resources**
Knowing how the labour market works Knowing how the labour market works	• Mediate with company HR personnel so they can grasp refugee realities. • Help refugees build their network through a range of networking activities. • Propose getting involved as soon as possible in activities that let them develop their skills and learn a trade (e.g., internships, integration activities). • Provide on-the-job follow-ups to facilitate communication with company HR to ensure everything is going smoothly. • Encourage employers to provide Francization courses to refugee new hires to help them integrate. • Practice several mock interviews, allowing for plenty of time. • Offer learning opportunities to discover the world of work in the host society and workplace language.	• Employment assistance organizations • Adult Education Centres (AECs) • Counsellors • Family and friends • Businesses and HR • Resources providing French courses in the workplace • Literacy and Francization in the workplace awareness brochures e.g., **La Littératie, un moteur de croissance pour l'entreprise et son personnel** • School service centres/ school boards
Knowing about employee rights and responsibilities	• Ensure on-going support with online job searches. • Maintain regular contact with the supervisor to ensure timely follow-ups on any problems arising on the job. • Introduce local, regional and provincial labour markets (e.g., types of jobs available, hidden job markets, required skills vs. preferred skills, work schedules). • Explain the basic information needed when starting a new job (e.g., bank account details, employer expectations, co-worker expectations, dress codes). • Advise about labour standards as well as employee rights and responsibilities. • Provide workplace health and safety training and documents in print form that refugees can refer to, with the help of an external resource or someone in their circle who can read (e.g., their children). • Create a list of the type of information that HR may request. • Ensure that refugees understand there are employment laws in place and that they can refer to them on the Internet or by asking for help from a resource person.	• *Labour Code, Act Respecting Occupational Health and Safety* (CNESST) • Counsellors • Businesses and HR • Employment assistance organizations • *Charter of Human Rights and Freedoms*

Employment Readiness and the Labour Market: Summary of Intervention Challenges, Approaches and Resources

Employment Readiness and the Labour Market		
Challenge	**Approaches for Counsellors**	**Resources**
Remaining employed	• Provide information about the realities of the job market and of the chosen field. • Plan for activities during training to help refugees identify and clarify their personal and environmental limitations, resources and needs. • Maintain regular follow-ups with employers to support refugee integration and HR. • Meet together with refugees and their supervisors at the workplace to review job performance and to better understand context. • Seize opportunities to explain to HR the realities of refugees in the workplace and any cultural differences that may be noted.	• Counsellors • HR management • Work colleagues • SOI teachers

7

Knowledge of and Access to Government and Community Resources

7.1　Main Challenges

- *Understanding How Institutions Work*

According to Marchioni (2016), "refugees often have difficulty grasping all the procedural aspects of immigration and at times are victims of wrong information" (p.23, free translation). This can not only cause extra delays, but also complicate matters. For example, a letter from the government is often not easy to understand (Clerc, 2019) and requires—especially for a refugee with little formal education—relying on a resource person with literacy skills. Having little formal education or a low level of literacy is therefore a major barrier to understanding how the host country's institutions work (Dezutter et al., 2018). Put together, all these administrative steps and hurdles can be particularly onerous for these refugees, who often find themselves overwhelmed by feelings of helplessness (Marchioni, 2016).

- *Knowing About, Understanding and Using Available Resources*

"[F]or some immigrants, the very notion of vocational guidance is foreign to them and the idea of making career choices new" (CSE, 2021, p.107, free translation). Added to the challenges of understanding the system is a lack of knowledge about available resources that could help with their SOI. That said, the varying lack of visibility of these resources and career guidance services is also sometimes to blame. A population survey (Bélisle & Bourdon, 2015) has shown that this is also an issue among adults without a diploma in Québec: only 15% of these adults who could use career guidance services "are [were] aware what organizations [could] help them answer all their guidance questions" (p.2, free translation). It is safe to assume that refugees are faced with similar challenges.

There are times, however, when refugees with little formal education do know about a resource or service they need, but still do not use—or feel comfortable using—them. For some, it is not easy to ask for help outside their family or inner circle (Arsenault, 2020) for a host of reasons. Some distrust public services and institutions because of past experiences. Sometimes they fear not being understood in French. To paraphrase Hanley et al. (2018), there is an absolute need for trust.

- *Developing Skills to Access and Use Resources*

In today's world, where online resources are used like clockwork to handle most administrative formalities, developing digital skills is inescapable for refugees with little formal education, who are often unaware of the existence or use of these resources.

> The frequent re-direction to online resources for getting information or needed services does not consider everyone's ability. The digital transformation occurring in Québec, in progress for several years now, is dependent on increased digital literacy [...]. Not only must you have the right equipment and Internet access, which are expensive, but also know how to use them (CSE, 2021, p.58, free translation).

Understanding how government structures function requires time for all categories of newcomers, who must, for instance, have an "understanding of the parts of the education system that concerns the schooling of their children or for their own needs, knowledge of codes, how the labour market works and its culture" (CSE, 2021, p.71, free translation). Coupled with language barriers, this lack of familiar points of reference contributes to making the entire administrative process daunting—to say the least—and reliance on other people. As one refugee pointed out, "Truly, there are lots of hidden things. We need someone at the beginning who can explain, direct, advise, welcome and support" (CSI, 2021 p.71, free translation).

7.2   Suggested Intervention Approaches and Resources

For refugees with little formal education, integrating into the host society hinges to a great extent on being familiar with and understanding available resources and services. While counsellors can help disseminate and explain many of these, there are two other elements they need to include in their interventions. First, they will most likely need to build refugee trust in public services. Second, they will need to adopt a pragmatic approach with various organizations to get them to clarify their educational and career guidance services for the target population and adapt how these are promoted among people with little formal education. Refugees who fall under this category would then be in a better position to understand the specific features of different employability programs.

The final table summarizing challenges, approaches and resources for intervention below is primarily derived from the work of Bimrose and McNair (2011), Dionne et al. (2022a), the Regroupement québécois des organismes pour le développement de l'employabilité (RQuODE, 2016) and a brief by the Conseil supérieur de l'éducation (2021). As with the previous sections, the approaches are drawn from an analysis of the experiences of people who work with refugees with little formal education.

Table 7. Knowledge of and Access to Government and Community Resources: Summary of Intervention Challenges, Approaches and Resources

Knowledge of and Access to Government and Community Resources		
Challenge	**Approaches for Counsellors**	**Resources**
Understanding how institutions work	• Ensure there is progress in learning the administrative language used in forms and applications—the types of questions they contain may confuse refugees (e.g., filling out the field "last address" can be an issue for those who spent years living in one or more refugee camps). • Ensure from the outset that refugees have the required documents to work; otherwise, swiftly take the necessary steps to rectify this. • Acknowledge that it is normal to feel discouraged in the face of administrative red tape and delays but stress the importance/requirement of having official documents to continue with the process or transition into employment. • Offer topical workshops on different parts of the system (e.g., how regional, provincial and federal institutions and structures work; available services and programs, general information about different government bodies; employee rights).	• Francization teachers • Francization programs • Community organizations • Counsellors • Family and friends
Knowing about, understanding and using available resources	• Encourage target searches on contacting relevant organizations (address, telephone number) so that refugees can get information verbally. • Provide computer support to access key contacts on government websites (municipal, provincial, federal). • Promote face-to-face contact to make communication easier. • Make yourself available to accompany refugees when they are referred to other services, to facilitate connecting with new people.	• Francization teachers • Francization programs • Community organizations • Counsellors • Family and friends
Developing skills to access and use resources	• Provide computer support for doing job searches. • Introduce text-to-speech features in different applications (e.g., Chrome or Safari web browsers, Google search engine, Word): choice of voice, adjustment of speed, language variations (French or Canadian French). • Embed computer courses in conjunction with vocational guidance. • Create client-friendly brief handouts with concrete examples.	• Francization teachers • Francization programs • Community organizations • Counsellors • Family and friends • Introductory computer courses offered by community organizations • Text-to-speech apps • AI

Part Two

Theoretical Models and Their Practical Uses in Guidance Intervention

1
Cultural Differences

In supporting refugees with little formal education in their career guidance and social and occupational integration (SOI), an understanding of issues underlying cultural differences is in order. Awareness of these differences allows practitioners to develop intercultural skills and better understand the environment in which the Other's world is built. This reference to the world of the Other provides critical information that deepens the concept of guidance intervention in general, and career guidance and SOI specifically, based on an intercultural approach.

Referencing the Other's world can help sensitize counsellors to the danger of interpreting the experience of the person in front of them through an ethnocentric lens—in other words, having the (conscious or unconscious) tendency to favour one's own ethnic group and using it as the only reference model (Cohen-Emerique, 2015; Kilani, 2014). Defined as conscious or unconscious biases that distort our interpretation of realities that differ from those of our own group, "Ethnocentric thought can also lead to a more negative opinion of foreign groups and to a superior view of our own" (Ma, 2022). Ethnocentric interpretation can also lead to the pitfalls of categorization and stereotypes, traps that systematically interpret the behaviours, values and skills of refugees based on one's own culturally ingrained assumptions. For counsellors, stepping into someone else's world is instead about committing to build their awareness in a considered, self-reflective disposition to interculturality. This allows counsellors to better reach out to refugees and understand their experience, access the meaning they give to this experience and their perception of their situation.

In Part Two, we will explore the concept of cultural differences through a discussion of seminal models, notably the one designed by Hofstede et al. (1994; 2010), and by including SOI-centric intervention approaches for refugees. Primarily intended for group interventions, these approaches are also perfectly adaptable to one-on-one support. In this case, it would be advisable to consider options such communal spaces to meet, for example, to bring clients out of social isolation, foster mutual support, share experiences and pool individual resources. In a similar vein, within group interventions, one-on-one meetings should also be included to provide each member of the group with a personalized safe space to focus on particular aspects of their case.

1.1   Understanding Cultural Differences Using Hofstede's Model

The cultural model pioneered by Hofstede et al. (2010) is helpful for understanding how different cultures around the world organize themselves. Hofstede originally created the model based on four dimensions, later adding two in collaboration with Minkov to arrive at the current six-dimension version: 1) Individualism-Collectivism; 2) Power Distance; 3) Masculinity-Femininity (referred to here as social gender roles); 4) Uncertainty Avoidance; 5) Long- and Short-Term career guidance; and 6) Indulgence-Restraint. Whenever the formulation of a dimension includes a contrast, Hofstede (2011) clarifies that each of the opposing terms should be understood as extreme poles of the culture and not absolutes. In reality, a country's culture cannot simply be defined as either/or; in his theoretical model, the cultures of the host country and the country of origin are more likely to be found somewhere along the continuum between opposing terms.

While applying a model such as Hofstede's in an intervention demands proceeding with great caution, counsellors may find it useful to deepen their self-awareness and knowledge of the Other's cultural characteristics. In the types of interventions discussed in the present guide, these characteristics refer to, for example, the values, attitudes and customs in the refugee's culture of origin and those of the host country. In their work, counsellors can thus draw on this understanding to become more mindful of their self-cultural determinants. They also become more vigilant of the impact these determinants can have on their perception of the Other (the refugee), and this can help them adopt an empathetic stance. Familiarity with these dimensions can also eschew ethnocentrism on the part of both counsellor and refugee. Simply put, counsellors will be better equipped to plan their interventions while respecting the Other's values.

For the purpose of this guide, we opted to examine three of Hofstede et al.'s six dimensions, selecting those we deemed most applicable to the integration of refugees with little formal education. We believe that for refugees, dimensions that overlap the spheres of education (individualism-collectivism), employment (power distance) and family (masculinity-femininity) pose a particular challenge to their integration into Québec society. The following sections describe of each of these dimensions, followed by an SOI-contextual analysis. This will help clarify cultural differences and expand on some themes up for discussion during SOI group interventions.[16] We conclude Part Two with suggested approaches for intervention where testing yielded conclusive results.

1.1.1   The Individualism-Collectivism Dimension

The individualism-collectivism dimension refers to the social integration of the individual into a group and characterizes the principles of membership to this ingroup; this membership can define attitudes and behaviours of those affiliated with it. In their model, Hofstede (1994, 2011) and Hofstede et. al. (2010) include a series of world maps detailing a breakdown by countries of this dimension's polar opposites. Some countries—Canada, the United States, Australia and several in Eastern Europe—are identified as predominantly individualist, while others—particularly some in Africa, South America and Asia—are found more on the collectivist side of the continuum.[17] Besson & Valitova (2021), however, have challenged some of the underlying principles applied to Canada's polarized categorization as a notionally individualist country.

The table below provides a summary of the broad characteristics of the individualism-collectivism dimension. Cultural differences specifically related to education, employment and the family are detailed in the three tables that follow, including links to practical considerations for SOI meetings and suggested intervention approaches.

---

16   These dimensions are also applicable to one-on-one meetings.

17   Hofstede's model maps can be viewed at https://geerthofstede.com/culture-geert-hofstede-gert-jan-hofstede/6d-model-of-national-culture.

Table 8. Broad Characteristics of the Individualism-Collectivism Dimension»
(Agodzo, 2014; Hofstede, 1994)

Individualism ⟵————————————⟶	Collectivism
People feel independent and make choices and decisions for themselves.	People know their role in life; their status is socially ascribed.
Individual interests take precedence over those of the group.	Group interests take precedence over those of the individual.
Individuals look after themselves and their immediate families.	Individuals are born into extended families or clans that provide protection in return for loyalty.
The right to private life is distinct from public life.	Emphasis is all on belonging to the ingroup (extended family, clan, tribe), since identifying with and belonging to this group are paramount.
A healthy mind is important.	Harmony must be maintained at all costs.
Transgression of norms can lead to feelings of guilt.	Transgression of norms can lead to feelings of shame.
The word "I" is indispensable in the language.	The word "I" is avoided and replaced by "we."

Table 9. Education in the Individualism-Collectivism Dimension

Cultural Differences	
Individualism ⟵————————————⟶	**Collectivism**
The purpose of education is to "learn how to learn" and prepare people to take their place in society among their peers: lifelong learning.	The purpose of education is to learn "how to do" so as to participate in society. School-based learning occurs during childhood.
Students expect to be impartially treated as individuals.	Students are treated as a group, not as individuals. Harmony and pride are dominant values; anything that runs counter to these can be experienced as shame for the group.

Education in the Individualism-Collectivism Dimension

Practical Considerations for SOI Group Training and One-on-one Meetings

- Refugees with little formal education emigrating from so-called collectivist countries tend to be more familiar with learning communally. In an SOI group, the support provided by counsellors and participants helps bring out the latter's resources and transmute them into opportunities for choices and achievements. This participation boosts the chances of achieving objectives and fosters mutual support and solidarity (Dionne et al., 2022b).
- Given that these refugees tend to learn communally and are concerned with concrete benefits for their ingroup (the "we"), they are less likely to be familiar with the concept of introspective exercises and/or individualized activities (focused on the "me").
- Members of this group tend to develop more "learning how to do" strategies, and many of them may have not had exposure with "learning how to learn" strategies. Those with lower levels of education also tend have challenges related to executive function (Gagné et al., 2009), which is defined as "a set of cognitive processes that develop from birth to adulthood, enabling individuals to intentionally regulate or control their emotions, thoughts and actions in achieving a specific goal" (Montminy & Duval, 2022, free translation).[18] Getting involved in the SOI group would have an impact on their cognitive development and, by extension, on their social integration (Dionne et al., 2022b).
- Refugees with little formal education from a collectivist culture are able to wait to take a position when they know the opinion of the group.
- In a case of individual need, all members from a collectivist culture may join forces to help out, regardless of the time this might take or their own interests.
- During conflict, people from a collectivist culture may feel ashamed about the lack of harmony in their group. This emotion is more associated with the experience of living together as a group than with individual experience.

Suggested Intervention Approaches

- Adjust to their learning pace, and structure exercises step by step. The people in the group are very tolerant and patient with those who have more difficulty.
- Repeat important concepts often, making links with employment and counselling at every opportunity.
- Include strategies for developing executive functioning skills.
- Gradually and regularly include introspection exercises by explicitly linking them with employment and encourage working in small groups rather than individually. Clear explanations of expected outcomes from the exercises can help hammer home why this type of activity is relevant (e.g., "being able to identify your skills can help you to prepare for questions asked during a job interview").

---

18 Some research has explored this point in relation to executive function (working memory, activating, planning and organizing, inhibition, cognitive flexibility and emotional regulation). To learn more, see:
- Gagné, Leblanc & Rousseau (2009);
- Teaching strategies for developing executive functioning skills, e.g., **www.teachspeced.ca/fr/fonctions-executives?q=fr/node/1161**;
- Executive functioning and refugees: Pocreau & Borges (2006); Chen et al. (2019).

Education in the Individualism-Collectivism Dimension

- Make learning concepts easier through practical exercises where participants help each other and share ideas. For example, in an SOI group, activities engage refugees and let them consciously and collectively think about their future, while still taking into account the affective aspect (Dionne et al., 2022b).
- Discuss the importance of expressing an opinion, especially when asked; create a culture of open dialogue, leading by example.
- Offer exercises to encourage the exchange of opinions and prepare participants for a job. Developing their ability to assert themselves, take a stance or give their opinion helps to empower them and encourages openness to different job opportunities (Dionne et al., 2022b).
- During group workshops, demonstrate the meaning and importance of knowledge to help participants better understand how they can use it in their decision-making when integrating into a job and remaining employed. Labour market knowledge acquired by refugees under an SOI program can help them land work (Dionne et al., 2022b).
- Promote the establishment of rules for the group, e.g., respecting and accepting differences in opinion, the right to make mistakes and learn from them.
- In a conflict, normalize and justify the learning of all parties to restore greater group harmony. The intervention can be used to share conflict resolution strategies and raise awareness about emotions felt during the conflict — and gradually work on them.
- Help group members, through frequent feedback, recognize their individual contributions to the group harmony and connect the dots between their personal resources and employment.
- Recognize the *I* through the *we* and the *I* for the *we*.
- Apply various learning concepts so refugees can expand their understanding of a given (at times complex) situation. (Dionne et al., 2022b.)

Table 10. Employment in the Individualism-Collectivism Dimension

Cultural Differences	
Individualism ← ──────────────────────── →	**Collectivism**
Hiring a family member is considered nepotism. In the labour market, the act of recruiting is regarded as a business transaction.	Employers hire individuals who are part of an ingroup, or are family members or relatives of other employees.
Companies, unions and associations serve as affiliation groups.	The workplace can, in turn, become an ingroup to identify with. Poor performance is no reason to be fired. The group will often pitch in—for example, a senior member will take responsibility for the mistakes of a junior one to avoid the latter being dismissed.
Management is individualized: incentives and bonuses are linked to performance.	Management is tied to group performance. A shared ethnic background can help smooth integration into the team.
In some industries, performance reviews are considered necessary to improve the quality of work. Open discussions with authority are valued.	Performance reviews are not considered, given that discussions between authority and subordinates would be tantamount to breaking the harmony. In the event of an issue, the family may need to get involved.
Carrying out a task often takes precedence over personal relationships.	Personal relationships take precedence over any task at hand.
Personal opinions are expected and welcomed.	To maintain harmony, opinions are those of the group.

Practical Considerations for SOI Group Training and One-on-one Meetings
• Consequences of certain behaviour exhibited during training or on the job can be interpreted as self-aversion or dislike rather than failure to comply with rules. • Some people see making mistakes not necessarily as something to learn from, but rather something to be ashamed of, having disappointed authority and the group. In cases like these, a group—primarily made up of members from a collectivist culture—might assume responsibility for those in difficulty by taking on their tasks and covering their mistakes. • During a performance review, those from a collectivist culture tend to listen and not engage in discussions. • People from a collectivist culture lean toward prioritizing social relations over work duties, which may be construed as tardiness and/or unproductivity. Faced with a person in need, they might find it difficult to understand why it is not incumbent on them to help.

- People from a collectivist culture seek to meet the expectations of authority and the group rather than individual ones, meaning that, for example:
  - Refusing an order from authority or the group can be considered impolite; as they do not wish to disappoint, they will avoid prioritizing individual expectations.
  - Asking about individual expectations or goals can be difficult if not impossible: these have to be set by the group—and even more so by authority—and not by the individual.
- In a collectivist culture, the opinion of the group overrides any personal ones. It thus goes without saying that at a roundtable, opinions are not likely to vary much from one person to the next.

Suggested Intervention Approaches

- Introduce clear operating rules for the group, including consequences for non-compliance. These should be made known to everyone to help understand this management method, depersonalize consequences and promote learning from mistakes.
- Take the time to check reasons for being late—it helps to understand refugees through the lens of their culture of origin—and explain the context of the host culture to build meaning.
- Prioritize an experiential learning approach. Give weight to self-evaluation of tasks, disclosing difficulties or owning up to a mistake. Learning from the latter is also important and should be encouraged.
- Regularly leave room for fun, humour and laughter to set a good mood. Among refugees, these quintessential sentiments can make them feel like they are part of a family; it compensate for the past when their social and educational life was disrupted by their migration (Dionne et al., 2022b).
- Organize team productivity exercises to help participants understand how one can take care of a relationship and still be productive.
- Teach about the different ways of communicating to help them:
  - Deal with the idea of not wanting to disappoint authority or the group.
  - Give an answer based on their personal preferences and conditions.
- Promote expressing personal opinions and the abundance of different points of view.
- Post large whiteboards on the walls for writing new words learned in context: acquiring language related to a specific concept can help them gradually become proficient at it, both intellectually and emotionally (ibid.).

Table 11. Family in the Individualism-Collectivism Dimension

Cultural Differences	
Individualism ⟵————————————⟶	**Collectivism**
In individualist cultures, the exchange of different opinions is considered part and parcel of the search for truth; conflict is a normal part of family life that	In most collectivist cultures, it is considered rude to confront someone directly as harmony in the environment is good for one and all. Group loyalty is essential and demands pooling resources.
Children are encouraged to form their own opinions; those who only parrot others' opinions are considered as having no personality.	Children learn and adhere to the group's opinion.
Children are encouraged to work a certain number of hours to earn spending money; missing out on family events because of work is accepted.	Family rituals are obligations in a collectivist family; attending family gatherings is extremely important.
Communication is verbal, social conversation is expected. There is seldom room for silence.	In a collectivist culture, being together is sufficient; it is not essential to talk.
Guilt is a personal feeling. It is felt by the individual irrespective of whether the act committed is known. Self-respect is a hallmark of individualist cultures.	Shame is a social feeling (not wanting to lose face). When one of its members has broken the rules, the whole group will feel the shame because the infraction will be known outside the group.
Family members need their own personal space.	Collectivist societies forge pseudo-family ties. It is common for several families to live in the same dwelling.

Practical Considerations for SOI Group Training and One-on-one Meetings

- People from collectivist cultures will not decline an invitation directly. For the sake of preserving harmony and loyalty, they will find an indirect way to turn it down.
- Many behaviours can be explained by the desire to avoid feeling shame, e.g., not admitting one's own (or someone else's) mistake, not being able to answer a question, not asking for help to understand or carry out a task.
- Sometimes it is hard to grasp the notion of work before family.
- In the group, and even in the workplace, people refer to others they know as brothers and sisters, and older people as mom or dad.
- They do not need their own space; knowing someone else is very close by suffices.
- Plan communication exercises on how to deliver messages directly and how they affect the other person. Acknowledge the value of harmony even when messages are direct.
- Explain the evolution of the labour market to show the meaning of the workplace in an individualist society.

1.1.2   The Power Distance Dimension (Relationship to Authority)

Power distance can be described as the expected and accepted distribution of power between individuals in a society. Comparisons based on power distance are useful in explaining or prescribing ways of thinking and behaviour. Besson and Valitova (2021) argue that, in Canada, power distance does not automatically play out along cultural lines but rather more on companies and businesses, depending on their target objectives and strategies. Low power distance is also noted, for example, in Germanic, Scandinavian, Northern Anglo-Saxon countries and Australia. At the other extreme, the cultures of Latin and Asian countries generally appear to be characterized by high power distance.[19]

As with the previous dimension, the table below includes a summary of the broad characteristics of the power distance dimension, followed by tables on the cultural differences in education, employment and the family that include practical considerations and suggested intervention approaches.

Table 12. Broad Characteristics of the Power Distance Dimension
(Agodzo, 2014; Hofstede, 1994)

Low Power Distance ⟵⟶	High Power Distance
Power is legitimate.	Power is a fundamental fact of society. .
Expressing one's ideas about power is valued.	Submitting to power, abiding by the rules and obeying authority are important; authority is valued and respected unconditionally.
The power gap places high value on rank and status.	The power gap between individuals is determined by age, generation, gender and status.
Interpersonal relationships are horizontal: peer-to-peer.	Interpersonal relationships are vertical—a hierarchical and authoritarian tendency is discernable.

Table 13. Education in the Power Distance Dimension

Différences culturelles	
Low Power Distance	**High Power Distance**
Learning is student-centric, where students can discuss and, in some cases, even argue with their teachers.	The high-power relationship between teacher and student reflects the social recognition of the former's higher status.
The quality of learning is regarded as being dependent on several factors, namely teacher/ student relationships, teaching/ learning strategies, student characteristics, etc. (Hattie et al., 2017).	The quality of learning is regarded as almost wholly dependent on the excellence of the teachers.

---

19 See: https://geerthofstede.com/culture-geert-hofstede-gert-jan-hofstede/6d-model-of-national-culture.

Education in the Power Distance Dimension

Practical Considerations for SOI Group Training and One-on-one Meetings

- Immigrants from collectivist cultures tend to trust the teacher, given that they recognize them as experts..
- At the outset, refugees expect teacher-centred formal instruction, with knowledge imparted primarily through lectures. For many, group discussions or exercises are not seen as learning opportunities through sharing ideas, but instead as a time for applying the teacher's instructions.
- Refugees from cultures where power distance is significant expect teachers to play the role of disciplinarians in cases of deviant action or behaviour.
- In a group made up predominantly of refugees from high power distance cultures, senior members can be called or implicitly identified as the group's mom or dad; their authority can be sizable and unchallenged by the group. Younger members show them great deference and would find it difficult to contradict or oppose them. Given their lack of experience, young counsellors starting out may feel less credible in the eyes of an older person: a diploma, however, can lend authority. In cases where these counsellors are (or have been) in a relationship, or have children, this can also be recognized as a sign of maturity and help them burnish their credentials.

Suggested Intervention Approaches

- Make the facilitation approach and teaching strategies explicit.
- Explain the relevance of the different facilitation strategies or active teaching such as teamwork, experiments, reflective exercises, etc.:
  - Show the importance of learning acquired through interaction with colleagues.
  - Nuance the role of teachers and highlight their other roles that go beyond imparting knowledge.
- Give feedback as often as possible on gradually developed skills in teamwork and sharing opinions, etc.:
  - Valider les interactions dans le groupe.
  - Validate group interaction.
  - Ask participants what they took away from the discussion.
  - Seize opportunities to discuss differences between the society of origin and the host society to help them develop a better understanding of Québec society and make sense of these differences.[20] Broaching these topics as they come up during group activities is relevant since the already-established context makes it easier to immediately respond to the need to understand and encourage more participation in the discussion.

---

20 For example: gender diversity, social gender roles (in a couple and in the family, in the education of boys and girls), the place of men and women in positions of power, acceptance of differences, the place of religion in their lives and our relationship with religion, elders in society, separation and divorce, youth protection services (DPJ), mental health, reasonable accommodations, racism, rank, current events, etc.

Education in the Power Distance Dimension

Suggested Intervention Approaches
• Refer to certain Québec values[21] on a regular basis at opportune moments; this makes it easier to understand how they are applied in everyday life and consider how participants see them, relate to them compared to their own, and derive meaning from them.

Table 14. Employment in the Power Distance Dimension

Cultural Differences	
Low Power Distance ←	→ High Power Distance
A person in a position of authority is considered an equal.	Superiors and subordinates do not see each other as equal.
Roles can be switched: subordinates can become superiors.	Relationships between subordinates and those in a position of authority are often charged with emotion.
Subordinates expect to be consulted.	Subordinates expect to be told what to do.

Practical Considerations for SOI Group Training and One-on-one Meetings

• For many people from a high power distance culture, respect for authority can mean:
  • Always doing what is asked at all times and never questioning instructions in the event of a problem.
  • Expecting to be given precise instructions on the work to be done and doing it even if tasks are routine, out of respect for authority. It would seem disrespectful to take initiative or do otherwise.
  • Not addressing authority directly during work for fear of disturbing them. For example, waiting after finishing a task for the superior to come and assign another. They will refrain from reporting an issue on the job for fear of bothering them.
  • Not turning to a co-worker to get or check some information for fear of disrespecting authority.
  • It is more challenging to gauge the quality of their own work, given that it is the authority who knows whether it was performed well or not.
• When working as part of a team, unless specified by the authority, getting instructions, orders or being corrected on how to carry out a task from another co-worker can be a source of conflict.

---

21 See: https://cdn-contenu.quebec.ca/cdn-contenu/immigration/publications/fr/GUI_Pratique_Valeurs_FR.pdf.

Employment in the Power Distance Dimension

Suggested Intervention Approaches

• Discuss the relationship to authority figures in participants' culture of origin and make links with the one in the host culture to help improve understanding. Discussing the differences and similarities helps the process of recognizing the Other and the connection between the two cultures (Dionne et al., 2022b). Those involved can expand their awareness and this can be empowering.
• Modelling the concept of the power relationship in the host society can start with:
  • Asking for preferences and suggestions as often as possible. The instructor's attitude toward participants will help them understand the stance of authority.
  • Making the authority experience explicit. Ask, for example, to explain the difference in response to a workplace issue between an HR manager in the society of origin and one in the host society.
  • Assigning roles to participants during teamwork, e.g., moderator, oversight, leader, production and management. The aim is to get participants to play different roles and develop communication strategies.

Table 15. Family in the Power Distance Dimension *(Agodzo, 2014 ; Hofstede, 1994 ; 2011)*

Cultural Differences	
Low Power Distance	**High Power Distance**
Children are treated as equal as soon as they are considered mature enough.	Children have to obey their parents and those older than them, whether they are part of the family or not.
The goal of upbringing is to teach children to be responsible and have their own experiences, learn to say no and gain a certain degree of autonomy.	Children are taught to be obedient. Independence is not encouraged and showing respect for parents is a fundamental virtue. Parental authority continues as long as the parents are alive.
The parent-child relationship becomes one of equals.	The father has the responsibility and authority to protect his family and spouse.
A child's gender is not generally used as a criterion for hierarchical distinction between siblings.	Duties and responsibilities at home are assigned based on a child's gender and age rank in the family.

Family in the Power Distance Dimension *(Agodzo, 2014 ; Hofstede, 1994 ; 2011)*

Practical Considerations for SOI Group Training and One-on-one Meetings

- When making decisions, refugees from a culture where power distance is significant often want to consult their family first, given relatives know what is good for them; they want to fulfil the expectations of their family circle, community, etc.
- A job is very important to support the family.
- The family's needs take precedence over other things.
- In addition to accompanying their children, one parent might also accompany the other parent to medical appointments, even if this means missing work.
- The husband might accompany his wife to an initial in-person meeting, to protect her, ensure what is good for her, and in some cases, decide on her behalf. He also might decide to intervene with HR management in the event of an issue.

Pistes d'intervention possibles

- Recognize dominant family values and the role each family member plays.
- Differentiate the implications of private (family, friends, etc.) and public life (work) and highlight the consequences of these on work.
- Discuss with the group the consequences of missing work to accompany a child when the other parent is available.
- Accept the presence of a spouse or parent at one-on-one meetings.

1.1.3 The Masculinity-Femininity Dimension (Social Gender Roles)

In Hofstede's model, gender roles that set individualist and collectivist cultures apart are attributed so-called feminine or masculine characteristics: modesty, tenderness and kindness are associated with women and assertiveness and the importance of material success to men. These characteristics are based on gender naturalization, which has been largely disputed in recent scholarship on social gender roles (e.g., Doray et al., 2020; Giguère et al., 2020). The authors of this guide are also very critical of such a naturalist view of gender. That said, it is nevertheless important to note that the attribution of social gender roles can have an impact on the SOI process of refugee women. Including this dimension here provides an opportunity to be cautious: counsellors should always keep in mind that they "are not dealing with a culture, but with individuals and groups staging a culture" (Cohen-Emerique, 1993, p.72, free translation).

Based on certain cultural and religious values associated with patriarchy (Castro Zavala, 2013) noted among many refugees, it is incumbent on women to preserve the family unit, do household chores and care for children. These multiple roles have an impact on the household division of labour and can represent an additional burden on the SOI of women refugees. In addition to this burden, these women are subject to mental overload, which can be amplified by all the above-mentioned responsibilities. And let us not forget pregnancies (sometimes unplanned) that can bring the SOI of refugee women to a halt (Dionne et al., 2022b).

In some cultures, gendered differences are also visible in the importance given to men's voices to the detriment of those of women and/or non-binary people. It is important for counsellors to be aware of this so that they can understand, for example, why during an SOI meeting a man would answer a question addressed to his wife. In practical terms, this means counsellors need to adjust their own cultural values and expectations of gender roles. In the above example, adequately understanding cultural specificity could help the counsellor gently prompt the woman to speak for herself without at the same time offending her husband. Counsellors must also keep in mind that possible contradictions (or even rifts) can emerge in refugee couples and/or families when women adhere to the principle of equality advocated— albeit not fully achieved—in Québec and in Canada (Castro Zavala, 2013).

In a guidance intervention involving cultural dialogue, openly discussing gender issues—which incidentally have also historically been used as a source of discrimination against refugee communities and immigrants in general (Bilge, 2010)—might be needed. The intervention can then provide an opportune and non-judgmental moment to discuss the range of culturally ingrained assumptions about social gender roles and encourage all group members to express their opinions on issues that affect them. Additionally, the context of guidance and SOI support can provide an ideal space for discussing gender representations that could limit job possibilities for women or men (Dionne et al., 2020). Influenced by these representations, refugees might not dare explore the possibility of pursuing certain careers or may even reject some occupations outright without giving them a second thought.

Given the abundance of scholarship produced on social gender roles in the wake of Hofstede's model (Doray et al., 2020; Giguère et al., 2020), we feel it redundant to include a table comparing and contrasting the masculinity-femininity dimension. However, practical considerations for SOI group training and one-on-one meetings and suggested approaches to intervention will be summarized in the table below, to provide a tool for counsellors working with refugees from a culture that values this gender-based opposition.

Table 16. Potential Impacts of the Masculinity-Femininity Dimension
(Agodzo, 2014; Hofstede, 1994)

Practical Considerations for SOI Group Training and One-on-one Meetings

- When making a decision about a plan or part of one, a refugee woman might want to first consult her husband to get his explicit approval.
- Power relations in a group linked to social gender roles can determine who has a voice or why some voices are valued more than others (men vs. women).
- Family responsibilities can overburden women, resulting in exhaustion that can be felt in the group and at work.
- Overseeing child caregiving and education can mean missing group or one-on-one meetings.
- The prospect of working in a non-traditional profession or job might sometimes be difficult to envision and is often met with surprise during an intervention: "You don't say! A woman/man can do that?".
- A so-called traditionalist (de facto heterosexual) view of family and couple relationships can spark some lively conversation in an intervention whenever other models or possibilities are mentioned.

Suggested Intervention Approaches

- Encourage discussions about the values both men and women share to help them become more receptive to potentially controversial topics such as gender equality.
- Either in a group or individually, talk about expectations related to acknowledging the voice of each person in the group.
- Lead a discussion on the long struggle toward equality for women in Québec and in Canada. Ask participants how gender relations are manifested in their culture of origin. If the working alliance permits it, nuance the public and private spheres.
- Discuss how gender can be a sensitive issue for some people they may eventually work with.
- Talk about job expectations in cases when an HR manager or supervisor is not of the same gender. Use short videos to inform about sexual diversity and gender issues.
- Acknowledge and provide strategies used by participants for sharing tasks as a couple that can help the SOI of each.
- In instances where a refugee proposes something that runs counter to gender equality, respond tactfully and with empathy to what they said and then start a discussion around equality standards previously presented.

1.2   Understanding Cultural Differences Using Hall's Model

In addition to Hofstede, we considered a second seminal model for studying cultural differences, developed by Edward T. Hall. Hall's model considers two dimensions: one temporal, the other contextual. The time dimension is useful for delving deeper into a person's perception of time based on his or her culture; the context dimension is an integral component of intercultural communication. These two dimensions are discussed at length in the sections that follow.

1.2.1   The Relationship to Time

In Hall's model (1976), time is defined from two different perspectives: its distribution or its division. Individuals who organize time by distributing activities tend to schedule one task at the time and are considered as having a monochronic culture. On the flip side, those who divide up their time are likely to do many things simultaneously and are considered as having a polychronic culture.[22] The process of distributing or dividing time also brings into play a third, spatio-temporal dimension, given that activities take place in a specific setting and environment that determine how it will function. In the refined model (Hall & Hall, 1990), time is also described in terms of a set of characteristics that vary from culture to culture: pace, accuracy, lead times and completion, timing, flow of information, speed of messages, chains of action, as well as perception of the past, present and future. Similarly, Brown (2007) also references the value of the present, arguing that people tend to live in the moment. It is often difficult for these individuals to envision their future selves, as they might think they have little control over the future.

Holding back envisioning the future is especially relevant among people who experienced life in refugee camps or lived day-to-day in survival mode (Massengale et al., 2020). It is little wonder, then, that refugees who find themselves in a country where time is perceived and managed differently than their own way of relating to time might have trouble finding ways to be organized and function compatibly with the requirements of the host society. It would involve a tremendous amount of learning to understand the new operating rules, integrating them and making them their own.

---

22 To learn more about how the countries are classified, visit **https://geerthofstede.com/culture-geert-hofstede-gert-jan-hofstede/6d-model-of-national-culture/**

Table 17. Broad Characteristics of the Relationship to Time (Hall et al., 1984, 2014)

Monochronic Time	⟵⟶	Polychronic Time
Time manages life: time for work, for education, for family, etc., organized around the tenet "one thing at a time." Time accurately determines and coordinates actions (e.g., time for discussion).		Within a given activity, it is possible to toggle between multiple spheres of life (multitasking)[23]. The emphasis is on the overall activity: there is no separation of time for work, education, family.
It is important to stay focused on the task at hand.		Interrupting someone during a task is accepted.
Efficiency requires working at a fast pace; otherwise, the clock runs out.		Time is an unlimited resource.
It is important to respect set schedules, deadlines and requests based on predetermined timetables.		Having to stop talking even when the subject is not closed, or stop an activity that is incomplete is inconceivable. What is important is finishing what was started.
		A person who adopts a polychronic view of time can change plans depending on the moment.
It is generally accepted for someone not to answer a question if they do not have the time.		It is considered rude for someone not to answer a question, even if they do not have the time.
A person arrives at work, settles in and begins working by completing one task after another.		A person arrives at work, and before settling in, goes to chat with co-workers on subjects that may or may not relate to work.
Many short-term relationships can be developed within the context of a given activity, some in other spheres of life.		Relationships are for the long haul. They can begin in one sphere of life and expand to others.
Time is concrete and defined by task. Dividing activities into smaller parts allows focusing on one thing at a time, but can also lead to a loss of meaning linked to the broader context.		People decide how they spend their time based on the needs of the moment and context.
Decisions are made depending on their medium or long-term implications.		Decisions are made based on their short-term implications.
Punctuality is a must.		Taking anywhere from a few minutes to a few hours to get ready for or complete a task is acceptable.
Appointments are arranged.		Appointments are of little importance since there are few schedules. What counts is to finish what was started.

---

23 "Multitasking" here refers to performing two or more tasks simultaneously during one activity.

Broad Characteristics of the Relationship to Time (Hall et al., 1984, 2014)

Time is source of significant stress.	Life is not managed by the clock and time is not stressful.
Information is compartmentalized and time-consuming to transmit.	Information flows fast and freely in the peer group and may be off limits to outsiders.

Practical Considerations for SOI Group Training and One-on-one Meetings

- Given there are no airtight boundaries between different spheres of life, refugees may see their interactions with counsellors as friendships or social relationships, and are likely to invite them as guests to a celebration or their wedding. If the counsellor turns down the invitation, it may be taken as a rejection.
- In general, refugees are task-focused, keeping the same pace throughout the day. Taking the time to perform the task well is a priority, even if this means being less productive. Interestingly, some HR staff have noted that while refugees appear to be slower in performing their tasks, by the end of the day, they have accomplished just as much as someone who is working quickly.
- Meeting the needs of family and friends is prioritized. Refugees will reorganize their schedules depending on the dictates of the moment even if this might mean being late or absent.
- Planning for the future can be difficult at the start of an intervention, given that refugees have experienced many traumatic events or hardships (see Part One). This compels them to live more in the moment.

Suggested Intervention Approaches

- Explain to refugees that there is a time for family and a time for work. Clarify that setting boundaries between various spheres of life is a cultural thing to ensure they do not to feel personally slighted if an invitation to a private party or event is declined.
- Initiate a conversation on the "benefits" of time (e.g., punctuality versus the time given to a loved one in need) in different cultures; stress the importance of understanding cultural demands and expectations in Québec when it comes to respecting time and holding down a job.
- Illustrate the meaning of productivity, performance and efficiency in the area of employer and labour market demands, not forgetting the importance of relationships by:
  - Carrying out speed and attention-to-detail exercises to help participants learn how to manage the two.
  - Explaining the reasons for appointments and why it is important to respect them.
  - Using the example of someone's absence or lateness, when appropriate, to help the group decide whether the reason given would be acceptable in a workplace situation.

Broad Characteristics of the Relationship to Time (Hall et al., 1984, 2014)

> • Gradually build the idea of future prospects through a process of refugees recognizing their skills, understanding employment opportunities and testing their skills in internships. Given that part of guidance counselling is helping participants plan for the future, this task may require longer-term targeted support.

1.2.2   The Relationship to Context

According to Hall and Hatchuel (1987), to gain an insight into the challenges of intercultural communication, one must also consider the relationship to context: "the meaning of words and phrases depends on the context in which these are expressed."[24] Hall and Hatchuel (1987) define context, qualified as either high or low, as the information available in the environment at the time an interpersonal relationship takes place. In a high-context culture, the message is pre-programmed or implicit and specifically intended for a given recipient and environment; the message conveyed includes a minimum of information. In a low-context culture, the information conveyed in a message compensates for gaps in context: in such cases, the information is direct and abundant.

The authors specify that the relationship to context has a strong cultural connotation. In fact, a person's representation (or perception) of a message's purpose is dependent on their judgment of the message's intention and the meaning given to that context. The facts observed also affect this representation, which can vary by culture of origin, experience and knowledge of some tacit ground rules, where words alone are not enough to understand one another. Rive & Roger (2014) also reason that lack of understanding in intercultural communication is often related to the type of context, either high or low. People from culture X are likely to understand or interpret what they see or hear in culture Y by relying on their own cultural stereotypes. It is at this moment that they might actually become aware of them, since "[...] behavioural systems are too complex [and] rules governing behaviour and structure of one's own cultural system can be discovered only in a specific context or real-life situation" (Hall, 1976, p.56).

Improving understanding in intercultural relationships requires being receptive to other meanings of the message's intention, which is feasible by calling into question one's interpretation based on one's own culture.[25] Take the case of an interaction between people whose references are associated with two different contexts, one low and the other high. Those from a low context might think that there is some information missing and that the speaker—from a high context—is holding out. Conversely, those from a high context might feel overwhelmed by the speaker, who is conveying far too much information, and can only focus on the essentials and not capture all the details.

Language proficiency is not the only challenge, then, in a situation involving intercultural communication. Context, too, plays a major role: it holds a host of meanings, in addition to the conscious and unconscious

---

24 The theories of Edward T. Hall – Institut fur Romanistik (uni-giessen.de), consulted 15-07-2022
25 We will expand on this in Part Three, which covers the development of intercultural competency.

perceptions of those who are interpreting the world of another. In the case of refugees already in the throes of acquiring conversational proficiency (speaking and being understood), contextual discrepancies can raise one more communication barrier. The expression "putting things into context" takes on vital importance and its application involves solid intercultural skills, at least from those who counsel these clients.

As with the preceding sections, the broad characteristics of the relationship to context are summarized in the table below, which is followed by a table on communication that includes practical considerations and suggested intervention approaches.

Table 18. Broad Characteristics of the Relationship to Context (Hall et al., 1987, 2014)

Low Context ⟵⟶ High Context	
Information is abundant; for this reason, it is sorted, organized and presented clearly and accurately.	Essential information is drawn from interpersonal relationships: people are well informed and maintain large information networks to be kept fully abreast of the latest developments.
Rules and contracts are explicit.	Rules and contracts are implicit.
Time is monochronic and structured.	Time is polychronic and malleable.
In the public sphere, people are more reserved. This is in contrast to their private life, where relationships are warmer and friendlier.	When meeting someone, people try to connect first, taking time to inquire how the person is doing, how the family is faring and engaging in small talk.
New people can quickly be accepted into the group.	There are strong boundaries between members and non-members of a group.

Table 19. Broad Characteristics of the Relationship to Context
(Hall et al., 1987, 2014)

Low Context Direct Communication ⟷	High Context Indirect Communication[26]
Gets straight to the point.	An attempt is made first to establish a connection to preserve harmony, and then discuss the goal.
Aims to convey as much clear information as possible to eliminate any misinterpretation, ambiguity or multiple meanings. .	At the time of the communication, there may be hints, suggestions, intentions or subtexts, which can leave room for interpretation
Allows to: · Mention the reality by name, even if it is potentially awkward or embarrassing. · Admit ignorance or difficulty. · Favour a direct answer, even if it may offend.	Allows to: · Mention the essentials of a reality that might be considered awkward or embarrassing. · Avoid humiliation when there is no accurate answer to a question or to conceal a problem. · Minimize having to give a direct answer that might offend. · Be polite and respectful of others and community life when making a request or giving feedback.

Practical Considerations for SOI Group Training and One-on-one Meetings and the Workplace

- Making a connection with others begins with small talk—it is important to first show interest in a person before getting down to business.
- Too many explanations or details can create more confusion than understanding.
- In instances where instructions or situations are misunderstood, it is typically due to language. Other times, however, the concept needs to be contextualized for refugees to understand better. In fact, it is quite possible that in their country of origin, the concept in question may not even exist, leaving them without a yardstick to compare to.
- Given that Quebeckers (a low-context culture) tend to communicate directly and get straight to the point, those from a high context culture might feel rushed, or take it as a reproach, a lack of interest in them or even as disrespectful.
- Conversely, when people from a high-context culture communicate, those from a low-con text one may try to understand the message more quickly, having the impression that the one speaking is not answering the question asked, trying to hide something or not being truthful.

---

26 Site https://gestion-des-risques-interculturels.com/risques/la-communication-indirecte-exemples-observations-et-reflexions/, consulted July 15, 2022

Broad Characteristics of Communication Based on Context

(Hall et al., 1987, 2014)

- People from high-context cultures are very loyal to the group—all members forge strong bonds and constantly try to control their emotions, as being part of the group takes precedence over individual self-expression. For the sake of maintaining harmony, speakers beat around the bush, masking their primary intention behind a secondary one, preferring to take a back seat rather than putting themselves at the centre of their speech. When asked what they think, they are less likely to reveal it to maintain cooperation.
- The reason behind conveying a partial message is to read the room and find out what listeners are thinking, so the message can then be tweaked accordingly. The speaker may be evasive so as not to hurt the other's feelings, and this can leave room for suggestions and interpretations.
- People from high-context cultures will in some cases blithely explain or omit specific contextual details, expecting the recipient to understand without making every detail explicit.
- In the workplace, if a person in a position of authority from a low-context culture asks an employee from a high-context one (in our case, a refugee) whether they had understood, the answer is bound to be a "yes" even when this may not be the case. There are two possible reasons for this: 1) They understood the gist of the information through their culture lens, even without possessing all the details; 2) They cannot say no, as it would be tantamount to disrespect to claim the person who explained it to them was wrong or inaccurate.
- At work, people from a low-context culture may find it challenging to work with colleagues from a high-context one as the latter will take time to establish a relationship before broaching the subject or starting to work, which might be difficult for the other person to decipher.
- Employees in high-context workplaces are used to being interrupted many times during their work; this great flexibility has an impact on respecting agendas, setting priorities and making decisions to execute changes.
- People in a high-context culture are very loyal to their employer and need to develop ties in the company; ideally, they like to often have time for conversations with the staff around them.
- Based on Hall's model and our own research and intervention experiences with refugees from high-context cultures, their most important workplace values can be summed up as: harmony, cooperation, respect for family life and faith, mutual support and connection with co-workers, topped off by salary and job security.

Broad Characteristics of Communication Based on Context
(Hall et al., 1987, 2014)

Suggested Intervention Approaches
• Before the start of a meeting, spend a few minutes with refugees and ask them how they and their family are doing, to strengthen the working alliance and human-centric relationship.
• Try as much as possible to bring up in conversation the context of the culture of origin and that of the host culture to help refugees recognize the many different ways of understanding and interpreting something. Ask them, for example: "If you were in your country of origin, how would you explain this situation?" or "How would you act if you were in your country of origin?" Then steer the conversation around the similarities and differences with the host country: "And here, what's different?" or "And here, how should one act?" Putting the country of origin in the context of the host country has an impact on refugee identity, since welcoming the Other is part of self-development.
• Seize opportunities to discuss different contexts of the host society to broaden their understanding.
• Use role-playing exercises to encourage conversation about different work-related contexts.
• Organize company tours, short-term internships (a few days) so that refugees can get a feel for the workplace environment, atmosphere, nature of relationships, types of tasks and pace of work.
• Develop role-playing exercises centred on communication by including diverse contexts of the host culture. .
• If you receive an invitation, be gracious. Before replying, you may want to focus on the goal

Part Three
Intercultural Intervention

In Part Three, we will supplement the information presented in Parts One and Two with four theoretical and practical guidelines for developing the intercultural skills of those who work with refugees with little formal education, and more broadly with people from other cultures. In our view, these guidelines are essential for expanding knowledge in guidance and counselling interventions and developing intercultural competency, and include intercultural stance, intercultural attitudes and skills, intercultural intervention and culturally responsive guidance.

1
Intercultural Stance

Guidelines for an intercultural stance are organized around a framework that provides a better understanding of integration based on acculturation and identity strategies. Throughout this section, we will include reflective exercises to give counsellors an opportunity to measure themselves both personally and professionally in an intercultural context using their perceptions and stance.

For counsellors, being familiar with possible strategies that refugees with little formal education use can provide a clearer picture of the acculturation process and a relevant angle on interventions in an intercultural context. It is thus fitting to introduce here Berry and Sam's acculturation strategies (1997) and Camilleri's identity strategies (1990) (taken up by Amin, 2012), which offer guidelines for understanding and explaining refugees' behaviours during their multiple transitions.

1.1 Acculturation Strategies

Sabatier & Berry (1994) define acculturation as "a change in culture resulting from contact between two independent and distinct cultural groups" (p.275, free translation). Acculturation strategies are an integral part of refugees' self-knowledge of their context. These strategies can give counsellors access to indicators for initial assessment, support them to adjust the intervention approach accordingly and help with ongoing assessments thereafter. They can also provide insight into positive or negative outcomes depending on the strategy (or strategies) refugees adopt. Those who work supporting culturally diverse people need to reflect on how they can better situate themselves when working with them. The following exercises can guide this reflection.

Berry (2001, 2000) defines the response to the complex factors at play by resorting to several acculturation strategies. Specifically, he identified four:

1. **Integration:** This involves preserving origin culture and identity while also maintaining contact with the host society. The values of both cultures are then blended. For Berry & Hou (2021), this strategy fosters a sense of belonging among refugees and contributes to their well-being;

2. **Assimilation:** This consists of leaving origin culture and identity behind and seeking to establish relationships with the host society by adopting its culture at the expense of the origin culture;

3. **Separation/Segregation:** "Separation" is when those seeking to preserve their origin culture and identity deliberately avoid interacting with the host society. If this lack of interaction is imposed by the host society itself, it is referred to as "segregation;"

4. **Marginalization or Exclusion:** This is the loss of individual cultural identity without the possibility of establishing any interactions or relationships with the host society, a scenario—considered dysfunctional—that could be the result of discrimination against or exclusion of the refugee.

> **Reflective Exercise 1: Acculturation Strategies**
>
> How comfortable am I with intercultural relationships? How much or little do I know? What are my assumptions and beliefs about certain ethnocultural groups?
>
> What is my intention when I'm assisting, for example, a refugee with little formal education who is from a culture different than my own?
>
> What are my views on refugees integrating into the host society?

Being familiar with these four strategies serves two objectives. First, counsellors can draw on them to gather information about refugees' perceptions of their own acculturation process. During assessment, this information can then help guide counsellors to intervene in refugee identity. Second, their knowledge will support developing the self-awareness of all parties involved and, at the same time, facilitate identifying possible rational or irrational beliefs and the presence of spoken or unspoken expectations on both sides.

The following reflective exercise is divided into two steps (A and B) and is designed to address the two above-mentioned objectives. It also encourages reflective practice and developing intercultural skills. On the one hand, this line of questioning ensures considering the acculturation strategy employed by refugees, and on the other, identifying the chosen strategies that will move the goalposts of integration nearer or further away. This identification also affects the counsellor's stance and intervention.

Acculturation Strategies (Berry et Sam, 1997)

Step A:
Please answer questions A1 to A4 with the first response that comes to mind.

A1. Do you think it is important to preserve one's cultural identity and characteristics?
- ❑ Yes
- ❑ No

A2.. Do you think refugees should retain their cultural heritage?
- ❑ Yes
- ❑ No

A3. Do you think it is important for refugees to establish relationships with the host society?
- ❑ Yes
- ❑ No

A4. Do you think that refugees should adopt the culture of the host community?
- ❑ Yes
- ❑ No

Step B:
After completing Step A, please answer the following two questions.

B1. In the matrix below, which of the four acculturation strategies best corresponds to the answers you gave in Step A?

		Maintaining the Culture of Origin: Importance of preserving one's own cultural identity and characteristics (A1) AND Acceptance of refugees maintaining their cultural heritage (A2)	
		Yes	No
Contact with and Participation in the Environment: Importance of building relationships with the host society (A3) AND Acceptance of refugees adopting the culture of the host community (A4)	Yes	Integration	Assimilation
	No	Separation/ Segregation	Marginalization: Exclusion and Individualism

B2. What influence do you think this strategy has on your intervention stance?

We suggest discussing these questions with other members of your professional team.[27]

---

27 For education interventions an integration strategy is strongly recommended.

1.2 Identity Strategies

For Bajoit (1999), building personal identity rests on an "existential tension" that seeks to balance or reconcile "on the one hand what I am (and have been) with what I'd like to be, and on the other, with what I believe others would like me to be" (p.69, free translation). Their complex situation means that refugees can find themselves simultaneously building or rebuilding their self while having to cope with imbalances triggered by internal and external changes. These changes generate tensions and conflicts with the functioning of their psychic structures and their relationship with social structures. Dealing with this situation involves building new references, which is something that demands restructuring the self and redefining the meaning of fundamental life choices.

> Migration is often an unsettling experience involving the loss of membership to the ingroup and the support of the community of origin. Challenges in adapting—dealing with new social and cultural ways of operating—are manifold and can strike a dissonant chord with those of the country of origin (Fronteau, 2000). These many cultural losses are further complicated by the identity negotiations of melding two different worlds of reference (Akhtar, 1999). Having been forced to abruptly leave their country unprepared, refugees might feel these losses and disruptions even more intensely. This may be compounded by pre-migration trauma, as a great number of refugees have been directly or indirectly exposed to horrific events linked to war such as torture, death, rape and/or other forms of violence (Kalt et al., 2013). Such traumatic experiences also undermine identity by inducing a relationship breakdown with the self, others and the meaning of life (Wilson, 2006). Acts of violence such as those perpetrated during socio-political conflicts shake the foundations of security, turn the world of reference upside down and compromise the sense of internal coherence, trust in other human beings and connection with others (Monroy, 2003; Rousseau, 2000; Sironi, 2007; Stolorow, 2007). (Benoit & Rondeau, 2022, paragraph 2, free translation).

Everything unfolds as if refugees tackling multiple changes in their lives are obliged to "reinvent themselves." To do this, they need to develop strategies we will expand on here, drawing on the identity strategies developed by Camilleri (1990). For this scholar, these "identity strategies appear to be the outcome of individual and collective processes based on adjustments made in light of the situations and goals expressed by the players. Three elements are required: the players, the situation in which they are involved, and the goals pursued by the players" (Camilleri, 1990, p.49, free translation). In her work, Camilleri has shown that a situation that undermines identity can push the victim to resort to two types of strategies: the first aimed at restoring a sense of self-worth, and the second seeking coherence by re-establishing unity of meaning.

Strategies to restore self-worth seek to gradually reacquire a positive identity in the host country in the face of an adverse situation. For some refugees, one strategy would be to assimilate into the host country's mainstream by distancing themselves from (or possibly rejecting) their own group to escape hurtful prejudice. Conversely, others turn to their community of origin as a protective shield against hostility shown by the host community or assimilation.

These strategies can also take the form of paradoxical behaviours, i.e., claiming affiliation with their own group while rejecting its values and practices, or—in extreme cases—aggressive confrontational behaviour based on an excessive and provocative claim about the prejudice propagated by the dominant group.

Strategies to re-establish unity of meaning are intended to lessen the impact of conflicting elements between characteristics of self and group cultural identity and those of the host country. Consequently, refugees might—depending on the situation—sometimes feel a tug toward their culture of origin, and other times toward that of the host culture (simple and pragmatic coherence). This search for coherence could also rest on more complex strategies that consider all opposing elements (in their own culture and the host country) to try to rationally resolve contradictions in the hope of better articulating and absorbing them. Strategies can also be aimed at tempering the dissonance created by identity conflicts by acting on the element believed to be painful.

2
Intercultural Attitudes and Skills

Counsellors play a facilitating role in refugee transition and integration (Abkhezr & McMahon, 2017), and help to build a bridge between the host society and the experiences of refugees. This mediating role is essential and demands a relationship of trust grounded in robust intercultural attitudes and skills.

2.1   Understanding the Other and their Culture

In research studies on listening in the field of professional help, understanding is considered to be an attitude associated with active listening. This takes the form of an inner predisposition and is exhibited through behaviours that convey a message to others that we are able to reach into their world and value what is important to them. This type of attitude is conducive to building and developing relationships of trust and is especially important when working with refugees with little formal education: to be effective in an intervention with a refugee population, counsellors are informed and strive to gradually learn more about the customs, values and cultural characteristics of this population. Understanding people's culture and experiences and getting acquainted with their value systems is a form of cultural empathy (Abkhezr & McMahon, 2017; Arthur & Januszkowski, 2001; Bimrose & McNair, 2011; Fouad & Bryars-Winston, 2005; Massengale et al., 2020; Vespia et al., 2010).

In this approach, which entails regularly checking to ensure refugees have understood and are at ease throughout activities (Gonzalez et al., 2018), it is important to shed hasty generalizations and focus instead on the singular experience of the individual. This benefits refugees by allowing them to better understand themselves and grasp the personal challenges they face as they integrate into the host society and the workplace. This also helps refugees feel valued (someone has taken an interest in them) and be open to the new and the unknown.

2.2 Knowledge of Underlying Issues in Cultural Differences

Building and maintaining working alliances with refugees demands much more than a better understanding of their cultural practices. In fact, it is crucial for counsellors to engage in an ongoing development of their own self-awareness and intercultural skills to rethink their own worldviews. It is by developing these skills that counsellors become better equipped to fully grasp other cultural references (Arthur, 2017; 2021). This will enable them, for example, to be mindful of their own internal tensions associated with cultural differences. Counsellors can then try to identify these tensions to improve the quality of their work. Training in cultural differences and values is therefore a must for anyone supporting refugees (Arthur & Januszkowski, 2001; Cedefop, 2014). The more counsellors operate within an intercultural stance by consciously reflecting on their practice, the more they will be able to instil confidence in the people who seek their help (Goyer, 2005). This way they will be able to better mind the pitfalls of assimilation and those related to their own unconscious biases.

2.3 Minding the Pitfalls of Assimilation

Multicultural guidelines developed by the American Psychological Association (2017) for practitioners working in an intercultural context are very applicable to those who work in interventions with refugees. Counsellors are in fact often exposed to the pitfalls of assimilation, wanting (consciously or unconsciously), for example, refugees to adopt behaviours and understand the concept of employment without first considering their culture or the resources they have brought with them. There may also be a tendency (conscious or unconscious) to overemphasize differences and judge another's culture unfavourably (those people, us). This sort of bias, which can be qualified as "ethnocentric," can result in wrongly or negatively interpreting the reality of groups different from one's own.

The trap of ethnocentric thought may lend counsellors a sense of superiority (Clayton, 2006). Carelessness in their reflection process could unconsciously emphasize relative differences in worldviews and lead to communication problems or a premature relationship termination (APA, 2017). It might also create diverse forms of resistance (implicit or explicit) to understanding or change and ultimately hinder the effectiveness of the intervention.

2.4   Minding Unconscious Biases

- *On the Part of Counsellors*

Unconscious bias refers to instinctively making quick judgments about a person or group without first having all the information needed to objectively evaluate a situation. It can inadvertently slip into counsellors' attitudes and influence their intervention work with refugees (Université de Sherbrooke, n.d.).

Social stereotypes are biases against a particular social group; those unaware of having or harbouring them can cause harm. In working with refugees, it is essential for counsellors to be cognizant of their own unconscious biases so they can adjust their attitudes and behaviours.[28] The reflective practice approach suggested by Cohen-Emerique (1993; 2007; 2013) and Camilleri (1990) can be of valuable help here.

- *On the Part of Refugees*

In the relationships refugees have with the world or with others, unconscious biases can influence the way they see themselves in the host society. These can manifest as cognitive distortions such as under- or overestimating their ability to get an education or enter certain occupations. There is a need, therefore, to create a space for dialogue and reflection about the challenges in supporting refugees to (considerably) increase their awareness of possible unconscious barriers to occupational choices or in the SOI process. Establishing this space may not, however, be that simple. For example, an intervention process could result in refugees becoming aware of the stigma or limiting aspects of being part of a minority group (Dionne et al. 2020), i.e., the daily experience of living with prejudice and discrimination, a negative perception of their group in the cultural hierarchy or doubt in the face of stigmatizing remarks (Flores, 2009). To meet the demands of this type of intervention, it is nonetheless important for counsellors to learn about issues related to immigration and refugee status, rights and equal opportunity (APA, 2017).

---

28 For more on the different types of cognitive bias, see: www.psychomedia.qc.ca/psychologie/biais-cognitifs.

3
Intercultural Intervention: A Reflective Practice Approach

There is an abundance of studies on refugees in a variety of fields (e.g., sociology, education, career guidance and counselling), yet few have focused on the challenges faced by counsellors responsible for supporting refugee integration, either individually or in a group. The research of Cohen-Emerique (1993) is one rare exception to this gap. This scholar has shown that in intercultural work, respect for diversity and tolerance are attitudes that need to be learned and developed. Although many of us think of ourselves as open-minded and tolerant of other cultures and diversity, our attitudes and behaviours do not necessarily reflect this self-image. Exposure to diversity—even more so when providing services to immigrants and/or refugees—can undermine one's own values and threaten identity.

Cohen-Emerique (1993) reasons that true openness to others—fully welcoming their differences—presupposes having an intercultural attitude. The prefix inter signals the "process of interacting" that forms the basis of recognition of the Other's distinct identity, which enters into a dialogue with one's self. As counsellors too have values, beliefs, conscious and unconscious biases, an intercultural attitude requires them to recognize and differentiate their own identity from that of the Other. This requires a change in stance, which puts the counsellor and the client on an equal footing. The challenge, then, lies in not only the Other's culture (e.g., the refugee), but also in that of the person providing the support: "much more emphasis should be placed on the relationship between the I and the Other, between me, carrier of a culture and subculture, and what the Other, acting as a mirror to my own identity reflects back to me about who I am" (Cohen-Emerique, 1993, p.72, free translation). An identity dynamic thus underpins intercultural intervention and this may trigger defensive and reactive strategies on both sides (Camilleri, 1990). This intercultural interaction lets people or groups come together in a specific and unique context to mutually give meaning to who they are based on themes whose backdrop is tinged with the subjectivity of the respective cultures.

Cohen-Emerique's body of work (1993) helps us navigate the complex nature of the intervention process of refugees, especially those with little formal education. Developing relationships in such a context goes beyond the simplistic principle that knowing the Other's culture or sharing the same ethnic background will suffice. Understanding these differences is certainly important, but not enough. It is worth reiterating that we "are not dealing with a culture, but with individuals and groups staging a culture" (Cohen-Emerique, 1993, p.72, free translation). Cohen-Emerique's (2007; 2013) diagram of intercultural interaction shown in Figure 1 is a good illustration of the complexity involved.

Figure 1. Intercultural Interaction Diagram (Cohen-Emerique, 2013)

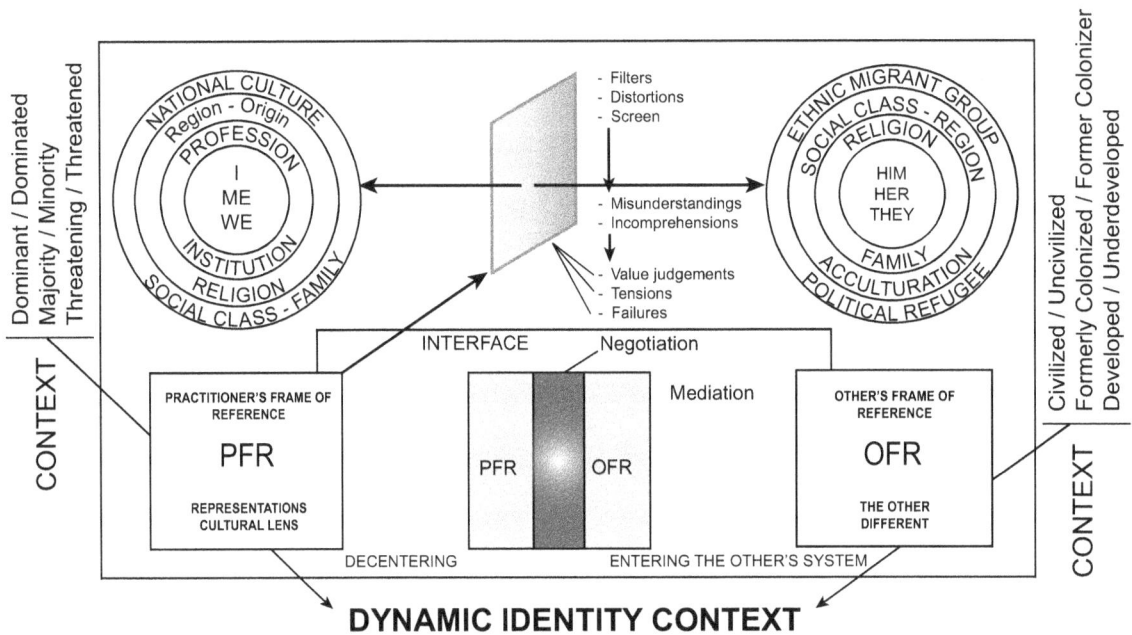

CONTEXT — Dominant / Dominated, Majority / Minority, Threatening / Threatened

NATIONAL CULTURE — Region - Origin — PROFESSION — I ME WE — INSTITUTION — RELIGION — SOCIAL CLASS - FAMILY

- Filters
- Distortions
- Screen

- Misunderstandings
- Incomprehensions

- Value judgements
- Tensions
- Failures

ETHNIC MIGRANT GROUP — SOCIAL CLASS - REGION — RELIGION — HIM HER THEY — ACCULTURATION — FAMILY — POLITICAL REFUGEE

CONTEXT — Civilized / Uncivilized, Formerly Colonized / Former Colonizer, Developed / Underdeveloped

INTERFACE — Negotiation — Mediation

PRACTITIONER'S FRAME OF REFERENCE — PFR — REPRESENTATIONS CULTURAL LENS

PFR — OFR

OTHER'S FRAME OF REFERENCE — OFR — THE OTHER DIFFERENT

DECENTERING — ENTERING THE OTHER'S SYSTEM

DYNAMIC IDENTITY CONTEXT

This diagram is best illuminated in the words of Cohen-Emerique (2007) herself:

The 2 squares correspond to cultural frames of reference, cultural representations or cultural lens (all equivalent terms used by different scholars) of these two identity carriers. They represent a matrix for interpreting events and individuals, produced by diverse allegiances and life experience and which are at the root of distortions and misunderstandings that interfere in communicating with the Other in an intracultural or intercultural situation. Distortions, however, are more amplified when players in the interaction are not from the same culture (Cohen-Emerique, 2007, p.15, free translation).

Reacting to differences always involves an individual dimension linked to a personal history or poorly resolved conflicts:

The hatched screen represents all the noise and barriers in communication on the side of the practitioner [counsellor] at the root of misunderstanding or the incomprehension in their relationship with the client [refugee], carrier of a different culture, noise which in turn will engender value judgments, tension, mistrust, and undermine the educational or support relationship.

The overall framework symbolizes the context that gets reset every time, that is, differences in status and disputes between people that the players involved represent. In addition to cultural differences, these players stage an often-conflicting identity dynamic.

The interface linking the two frames of reference with a line refers to research produced by the Palo Alto School, namely by Hall (1990) that studied how to make two cultural frames of references communicate by finding a language common to both. As a result, they pioneered interface concepts such as *proxemics, monochronic vs. polychronic time, high-context vs. low-context culture*, concepts that make cultural differences easier to understand and put into perspective, hence the importance of this school in the field of interculture. *Lastly, the diagram not only captures the complexity of the intercultural relationship and communication, but also helps us to identify how to overcome it:* through an intercultural approach and intercultural competency, as shown below the two frames of reference (decentring and entering the other's frame of reference) and at the centre of the diagram where the two frames meet (negotiation and mediation) (Cohen-Emerique , 2007, p.15, free translation).

For Cohen-Emerique (1993, 2007), the complex nature of intercultural interactions demands developing target skills to meet the challenges of "cultural diversity." Given that an interaction can indeed be at the root of misunderstandings, incomprehension, tensions and setbacks in the guidance process, she suggests adopting a reflective practice approach. Thus, when counsellors find themselves dealing with critical incidents or at a relational dead end, they can turn to her three-step approach to guide their reflection: 1) *Step outside yourself*; 2) *Listen and immerse yourself in someone else's world; and* 3) *Negotiate meaning to foster mutual understanding and comprise* (Cohen-Emerique, 2007, pp.17-19, free translation). These three steps are described below.

3.1   Cohen-Emerique's Reflective Practice Approach in Three Steps

1) Step Outside Yourself

Described as the act of *decentring*, this step is intended to help support workers better define their own sociocultural identity and be wary of first impressions, which are often laden with assumptions and possibly biases. It is a process that consists of "becoming aware of one's own frames of reference as an individual with a culture and subcultures (national, ethnic, religious, professional, institutional, etc.)" (Cohen-Emerique, 2007, p.16, free translation). It also comprises awareness of one's own *"sensitive areas"* (ibid.).

Influenced by their own culture and values that are important to them; counsellors may harbour certain preconceived ideas about other cultures. Consequently, depending on the origin of the refugees they are working with, they may hold some unconscious beliefs that can colour the way they sense and understand the refugee's words and behaviours. There may also be times when they are shocked. Self-awareness here is not about self-effacement, but "the opposite: it is a managed recognition that can help [them] to know [themselves] better and put into perspective [their] own values compared to others" (ibid., free translation). To develop this approach, it might be useful for counsellors to regularly assess situations that have, for example, clashed with their own values. This would help to clarify what this issue can reveal about their own culture, gauge the effect it had on their intervention stance and decide how this new awareness could be used constructively.

2) Listen and Immerse Yourself in Someone Else's World

Immersing oneself into someone else's world means moving toward it and having the ability to know that person from the inside—"putting yourself in someone's else shoes," as the old saying goes. To do this requires taking the time to be interested in them as a person, inquire about their situation and world-view, and lend them an ear; in other words, understand them. This hinges on an attitude anchored in the preceding step, as:

> To understand [,] is first of all, to decentre or step outside yourself and placing yourself in the other person's point of view; it is an attitude of openness, of marshalling cognitive (observation, desire to learn) and affective (non-verbal communication, allowing emotions to rise to the top) resources to discover what gives meaning and value to the other person (ibid., p.17, free translation).

It is through reflective practice that counsellors can effectively achieve these objectives, which necessitate stepping outside oneself and moving past offensive language to join the other person in their reality. This process of decentring and re-centring toward the other person allows cultivating a caring attitude for others (here, a refugee), and discerning the meaning they give to their cultural references. It promotes a deeper awareness of one's own biases and adjusting one's working assumptions. Brunel (1989) points out that the risk of biased interpretations is reduced when each person is aware of their own history and culture, as well as the history and culture of the other person. This constructivist approach to cultural empathy is ultimately grounded in recognizing similarities to bridge differences and minimize the impact of subconscious biases.

3) Negotiate Meaning to Foster Mutual Understanding and Compromise

What happens when integration is the subject of different points of view, representations or behaviours on both sides? This type of challenge demands establishing a genuine negotiation process on both sides that does not favour one culture over another. Otherwise, there is a real risk of falling into the traps of assimilation or separation.[29] There is then a search for compromise, for shared meaning that includes aspects of both worlds. This quest is intercultural mediation, and is made possible through reasoned examination of two competing rationales, avoiding absolute truths and making mutual concessions to "co-construct" representations of the same reality, perhaps even cultural co-creation.

> In terms of social and educational practices, this new social contract translates into a case-by-case negotiation approach, i.e., searching together (the practitioner and the migrant family) through dialogue and exchange a baseline agreement, a compromise in which each party sees their identity and core values respected, at the same time drawing closer to one another[...] (Cohen-Emerique, 2007, p.19)

Mediation can thus create a common space that benefits all parties over the long term.

---

29 See Part Three, Section 1.1: acculturation strategies.

3.2 An Example of the Reflective Practice Approach

Case Scenario

Lalla is a refugee with little formal education doing a work placement in housekeeping. Her supervisor is full of praise for her: she's punctual, diligent and hard-working.

When Lalla meets with her counsellor for a follow-up, she says she wants to quit her job, because another co-worker is always redoing her work behind her back and telling her she's not doing what she's supposed to do. Lalla doesn't dare say anything because she doesn't want to create problems, and she doesn't want to tell her supervisor for fear of losing her job. She'd like her counsellor to do it for her.

Step 1: Step Outside Yourself

Developing responsibility and independence among clients is a valuable part of a counsellor's job. In this respect, part of the purpose of guidance and counselling is to provide refugees with tools and lead them through their own efforts. In assisting this population, it is important to keep in mind that some may not be familiar with the customs and practices of the host country, that they are still learning a new language, and so on.

In this scenario, the counsellor could interpret Lalla's reticence to talk to her co-worker or supervisor as a lack of independence. A first reaction might be to encourage Lalla to be more independent by getting her to speak directly with the co-worker and the supervisor to clear up any possible misunderstanding and come up with some understanding on how the teamwork is to be carried out. However, decentring here would help differentiate the counsellor's own cultural bias (the importance of being independent) from Lalla's cultural bias (maintaining harmony).

Bearing in mind the possible communication and cultural barriers that Lalla could be facing, the counsellor reconsiders their original intention and opts to undertake a reflective practice approach to gain a better insight into Lalla's world. This is Step 2.

Step 2: Listen and Immerse Yourself in Someone Else's World

Immersing oneself into someone else's world means knowing that person from the inside—that is, focusing first and foremost on them as a person, their perceptions and their conflict resolution strategies. In our scenario, the counsellor could, for example, try to determine whether Lalla has had a similar experience before and ask her what she did to resolve it or how conflicts are managed in her culture. By leading Lalla to engage in introspection using her own experiences and representations, the counsellor is not only entering into the other's world but also instigating awareness of cultural references, and is now better equipped to understand the other person's subjective world while strengthening their own cultural empathy. They can then adjust their intervention beginning with these similarities and differences between the two cultures.

By taking on an attitude focused on understanding Lalla's world while being cognizant of their own, the counsellor allows Lalla to broaden her view of conflict management. The two can now spot cultural similarities and differences and pay attention to the presence of any ethnocentric slant in the intervention on both sides. The counsellor might learn, for example, that where Lalla comes from, conflicts are often dealt with by a person of authority or a third party acting as a mediator.[30] This change in stance helps the counsellor better understand Lalla's expectations of them and become aware of the adjustments needed. In Lalla's eyes, the counsellor, in a support role, represents an authority figure who has the right to intervene on her behalf in resolving the conflict.

In recognizing the similarities and differences between these two points of view, the counsellor recalibrates their interpretation of the situation and begins to negotiate meaning to foster mutual understanding and comprise. This is Step 3.

Step 3: Negotiate Meaning to Foster Mutual Understanding and Compromise

Now familiar with Lalla's cultural representations, the counsellor at this stage will name their own cultural representation and explain its meaning. This mediation enables identifying similarities and differences and beginning a co-construction of meaning.

A first option would be for the counsellor to explain to Lalla that they would be willing to speak directly to her supervisor; however, Lalla should first try resolving the conflict herself by talking to her co-worker about her concerns. This could help the two workers come to a mutual understanding and resolve the situation themselves. This is one way to encourage expeditious conflict resolution for the sake of maintaining harmony and confidentiality: two parties solving the issue on their own before escalating to a third.

Considering Lalla's standpoint, there is a second option that calls for a different approach, where the counsellor talks to Lalla about what the two cultures have in common when it comes to congenial interpersonal relationships. The conversation could also revolve around how this is done. During the conversation, the counsellor could also let her know that they understand the importance placed on the role of authority and Lalla's reticence to break the harmony with her co-worker. It is through this type of exchange that a shared meaning can emerge where Lalla can identify and develop with her counsellor a strategy that could work for her.

As a complement to the second option, the counsellor might also want to meet with or talk to Lalla's supervisor or co-worker to help Lalla develop her identity strategies. This intervention may risk being seen as infantilizing (by the supervisor, for example), but this is more about building and negotiating meaning where conflict resolution involves concessions between two cultural referents. In this process, Lalla will integrate new knowledge that can help her better understand the host society and its issues, as well as conceive integrated conflict-resolution strategies. When negotiating intercultural interventions such as these, we suggest counsellors try applying Cohen-Emerique's (2013) three-step reflective practice approach, shown in the table below.

---

30 See sections in Part Two on power distance (1.1.2) and the relationship to context (1.2.2).

Table 20. Cohen-Emerique's (1993, 2013) Reflective Practice Approach in Intercultural Interventions[31]

Regularly assess the effect of your intervention on its objectives and relationships with the refugee.

Step 1: Step Outside Yourself: Become aware of your own cultural references to recognize your cultural biases and the intentions of your intervention

- Describe the intervention (carried out or planned) and its real or potential impact on the other.
- Identify and explain the intention behind this intervention.
- Analyze the intention to detect any bias due to your own cultural referents.

Step 2: Listen and Immerse Yourself in Someone Else's World: Recognize and gain access to the other's point of view

- Describe what you noted about the other's worldview during the intervention.
- Examine what may have been retained from their perceptions of their own culture.
- Identify, if applicable, remarks that may have offended your personal values, representations or any other cultural referents.

Step 3: Negotiate Meaning to Foster Mutual Understanding and Compromise: Co-construct a shared meaning that considers cultural differences and context

When dealing with a situation marked by divergent points of view, it might be a good idea to ask yourself the following questions:
- What is the intended intervention and why?
- What are the similarities?
- What are the differences?

---

31 A logbook can also be used, if needed, to better assess the effects of the intervention on the relationship and the objective of this approach.

4
Culturally Responsive Guidance

Nancy Arthur and Sandra Collins' Culture-Infused Counselling model (2014, 2017, Arthur, 2021) is built on the principle that cultural identity contexts need to be taken into account when supporting individuals whose cultural values differ from those of the host society. Developed by these two Canadian career guidance and counselling scholars, this model is based on a constructivist approach. It can also be applied to understand how individuals develop their worldviews through personal socialization, which in turn shapes beliefs, values and expectations regarding the social norms of interaction. In this conceptual framework, Arthur (2021) suggests counsellors consider four core competency domains in which they can hone their intercultural competency, which is deemed foundational in supporting the integration process and bolstering cultural identity, values and characteristics of both the country of origin and the host country. We present these four core competency domains below, illustrated by two practical vignettes.

4.1 Four Core Domains for Developing Cultural Competency

Domain 1: Awareness of Personal Cultural Identities

Whether consciously or unconsciously, the culture and personal social values of counsellors shape their interactions with the refugees they support. Becoming aware of this is essential in interventions with people from diverse cultures. It is also important to cast a critical eye on the different foundational theories and models used in guidance practices, as most are based on Western European and/or North American worldviews.

Domain 2: Awareness of Others' Cultural Identities

Having a general knowledge of someone's else culture does not define that individual. That said, this knowledge can be enlisted to conceptualize preliminary working hypotheses and better understand how context influences personal values and behaviours. What remains first and foremost, however, is focusing on the refugee as a person to grasp their worldview about their career and SOI.

In the nexus of becoming aware of one's own cultural identity and that of another lies one of the top challenges in intervention in an intercultural context: overcoming ethnocentrism. For the counsellor, the pitfall of ethnocentrism is attempting to get refugees to act and think as they expect and to share similar values, which can be summed up more bluntly as a desire for them to assimilate. To steer clear of this, counsellors should opt for an approach where the two parties can explore their respective worldviews. This can help strike a working alliance—on both objectives and tasks—and an emotional connection.

Domain 3: Understanding Cultural Influences on Working Alliances

Many environmental considerations—location, hours of service, office furnishings—help create an atmosphere conducive to working alliances, but it is active and empathic listening for a human connection that enables trust and setting desired goals and activities. Openness to learning about someone else's culture leads to a better understanding of the influence cultural context has on refugee identity. This openness, buttressed by an empathy reflex, can in turn help people feel more at ease and open with others as they interact during the process.

Domain 4: Delivering Culturally Responsive and Socially Just Career Guidance

It is important that counsellors look at how refugees are personally affected by social and organizational systems. Obstacles or barriers affecting their daily lives or SOI can be examined through the lens of social justice. Counsellors can serve as advocates (Supeno et al., 2020) to help refugees better manage these challenging situations and make a positive difference, by marshalling their support network to take part in redressing injustices with them and on their behalf. They can advocate with authorities to lower or even bring down structural barriers in the refugee person's SOI or counselling.

Inspired by Arthur's model (2021), the self-assessment exercise in the table below applies the four core cultural competency domains and can be used to analyze intervention cases in an intercultural context.

Table 21 : Self-Assessment Exercise for Developing Cultural Competency

Case Description
Begin by describing an intervention case.

Domain 1: Awareness of Personal Cultural Identities

Meeting someone from a different culture can trigger awareness of differences and similarities with one's own.
Recalling the intervention case you just described,
- What aspects of your culture did you become aware of during this interaction (e.g., personal values, representations)?
- What challenges you in this new awareness?

Domain 2: Awareness of Others' Cultural Identities

In hindsight,
- Were you able to grasp the fundamental elements of the other person's cultural identity?
- Were you able to notice any specific aspects of their perceptions of their cultural group?
- Did you tend to lean toward generalizations or biases (e.g., stereotypes)?

Domain 3: Understanding Cultural Influences on Working Alliances

In analyzing the intervention process:
- Were you able to establish a good working alliance because of your ability to accurately reflect the other person's world?
- If yes, name what is important and central to the worldview of the other person.
- If no, what might have prevented it and how could you address it?

Domain 4: Delivering Culturally Responsive and Socially Just Career Guidance

If there is lesson to be learned from this case in terms of social justice,

- What might your role be?
- What social contribution could you make to improve some aspects of organizational structures or social systems?

4.2   Developing Cultural Competency: Two Practical Vignettes

To illustrate the practical application of the four core competency domains found in Arthur's Culture-Infused Counselling model (2021), we offer two vignettes created from real-life guidance cases with refugees.

Vignette 1

This first vignette features one counsellor's experience during an internship follow-up with a refugee. In the comments section of the intern's performance, the supervisor wrote that *"once she completes a task, she sits doing nothing, waiting for the next one. I find her too passive..."*

Let us examine this comment through the lens of Arthur's four domains.

Domain 1

In reading such a comment, the counsellor becomes aware of their "personal cultural identity" as a native Quebecker, which might characterize the refugee's behaviour as a "lack of initiative."

Domain 2

This new awareness gives the counsellor an opportunity to decentre and try instead to parse the refugee's logic. Withholding judgment, she proceeds to ask questions in an effort to understand the meaning of her behaviour. What the counsellor discovers is that in this refugee's culture, waiting for an order is considered a sign of great respect for authority. The refugee's reasoning is based on the fact she does not want to discredit the person who employs her (the authority) by presuming she knows what to do and doesn't need a boss to tell her, which in her culture would be a sign of disrespect. This misunderstanding perfectly illustrates the importance of recentring the refugee to access their worldview. Only then it is possible to develop, based on this foundation, effective strategies to facilitate refugee integration and job retention.

Domain 3

Rather than pigeonholing her in a category that inflames biases, the inclination of the counsellor to learn more about the refugee's worldviews helped them get a better grasp of cultural influences on employee identity. It also helped strengthen the working alliance and develop a solution co-constructed by the parties involved (refugee-supervisor-counsellor).

Domain 4

This vignette can also be used to illustrate how an intervention can be culturally responsive and socially just. Able to assemble the best conditions for a mediation intervention by decentring and understanding the intern's representation of their relationship with authority in the workplace, the counsellor was in a position to help all involved parties apply working assumptions conducive to a fair and respectful integration of diversity in the workplace.

Vignette 2

The second vignette spotlights aspects directly related to the counsellor's subjective world. In this scenario, a female refugee lets her counsellor know that she will need to first get approval from her husband before accepting an internship she has been offered.

Domain 1

As a person with feminist values, the counsellor was offended, and her first reaction was to tell the refugee she should be able to make her own decisions. Then, realizing the limiting effects of "her own cultural identities," she pulls herself together and turns to the refugee in an effort to understand her situation better.

Domain 2

The counsellor then asks the refugee why she would need to first get permission from her husband. The woman explains that important decisions are left to the head of the household, who happens to be her husband. It is up to him to decide what is best for his family, and what he says goes. That's the way it is, and for her, this is perfectly norm

Domain 3

In this vignette, we see a counsellor whose personal cultural value of gender equality has been affected. In her spontaneous reaction to the situation, she saw a refugee with limited decision-making power. After realizing her own position, she was able to start a conversation with the refugee about the role women and men play in decision-making in their respective cultures. This helped restore and maintain the working alliance. Building on this, she was able to make inroads, helping the refugee to understand and learn more about the role of women in the host society, how this came to be through historic struggles to achieve rights and the tangible gains women now get to enjoy in their everyday lives (e.g., having their own bank account, receiving family allowances, having and exercising the right to vote).

**Reflective Exercise 4:
Developing Cultural Competency**

If you are a counsellor working in a multicultural setting, you most likely will have experienced a situation similar to either of the two vignettes above.

Does a particular situation come to mind?

In hindsight, try to analyze this situation using Arthur's four core domains.

As part of your role you must manage many situations as an advocate (Supeno et al., 2021). How can the different models help you leverage more resources to redress social injustices?

Domain 4

The goal here is not to show that what happens in the host society is the perfect paradigm. It is instead about a form of intercultural sharing that aims to enhance mutual understanding. This helps to shore up trust and help the refugee realize the implications of the differences between her worldviews and those of the host society. She can then develop her own informed strategies to deal with them. In this process, the counsellor can also learn about these strategies and adapt her support accordingly.

Part Four

Intercultural Interventions in the Educational and Career Guidance Process

As elaborated in Parts One through Three, the development of intercultural attitudes and skills is becoming a necessity in counselling refugees in their career guidance and social and occupational integration (SOI). In fact, working with people from diverse cultures demands understanding the influence of personal and cultural identities and being able to take proper account of these throughout the process. This understanding becomes even more complex when the people receiving the support have little formal education and cannot speak the language or are unfamiliar with the cultural references of the host society—which can vary by community or region. An informed consideration of this complexity in intervention practices is an integral part of guidance in an intercultural context. In fact, it makes it possible to practise ethically and effectively. The efficiency of such interventions rests on:

a. Establishing and maintaining a strong working alliance in a safe intervention built on a two-way dialogue between cultural identities (counsellor and refugee);
b. Recognizing that interculturality and diversity require a continued commitment to develop increased awareness, knowledge and communication;
c. Supporting the development of career management skills.[32]
d. Considering intercultural matters throughout the guidance intervention process converts them into sources of ongoing reflection for improving communication and co-constructing balance strategies best adapted to the reality of each individual that a counsellor supports (Goyer, in press).

In Part Three, a number of theoretical guidelines and their practical implications revealed the wide range of learning and development of targeted skills required to provide guidance to people in an intercultural context. This is evidenced in the field by many counsellors who sometimes find themselves ill-equipped, especially when new to their practice and faced with the many challenges that come with practising their profession in such a context. To offer substantive answers to the fundamental questions of ethics this raises, the first section of Part Four is devoted to increasing awareness of some of the challenges that require careful consideration in rethinking guidance practice when working with refugees with little formal education. With this in mind, some specific aspects of the guidance process will then be discussed. Part Four is then rounded off with a presentation of suggested approaches for intervention based on practical experiences for each of the phases of a proposed guidance process.

32 Michaud (2003) defines these skills as "the ability (know-how) of a person to leverage their resources related to their career guidance [...] personal resources often refer to personality, intellectual, cognitive and affective functions [...] leveraging personal resourcing [represents] the subjective and intersubjective organization of interests, values, aptitudes, beliefs and behaviour patterns at the affective, cognitive, somatic, behavioural, relational and contextual levels" (pp.86-87, free translation).

1
Key Aspects of the Guidance Practice for Refugees with Little Formal Education

In Part One, we showed how the practice of counselling refugees requires addressing the particular challenges experienced by these clients. In such a context, it becomes necessary to reconsider several fundamental aspects of guidance, namely free and informed consent, assessment and labour market information (LMI).

1.1   Free and Informed Consent

The very principle of free and informed consent in the context of providing support to refugees with little or no formal education raises some fundamental questions: What exactly does free and informed consent mean for this group of refugees? How do they perceive the role of the career counsellor? And can their consent, in fact, be truly informed when their understanding of the language and the principle of consent itself are fuzzy? These questions all point to the need for adjustment. This adjustment should include, but not be limited to, the language used in consent forms, how they are presented and the role of the counsellor. In fact, obtaining truly free consent requires transparency about ramifications of a "yes" or "no" answer. For example, it is quite feasible that some refugees will automatically agree to anything proposed to them simply out of fear of losing out on resources for themselves and/or their family (e.g., allowance, support, network). In such cases, can we really call this consent "free"? Rather, this consent is more likely the case of an administrative requirement conditioning access to resources—hence the importance, in our view, of focusing instead on potential benefits and drawbacks. In this way, individuals have the possibility to make an informed choice—albeit constrained—and articulate the concerns or fears that determine their answers.

Some adaptations to consent forms could include, for example:

- Defining the main concepts used by contextualizing them and using translation tools to translate any unclear concepts into the refugee's language;
- Doing everything possible to ensure the meaning of consent is clearly understood by providing approximations with similar practices in the cultural references of the refugee;

- Opting for gradual, oral consent that would help properly explain the meaning of the term in the helping professions in the host society. In some cases, understanding consent is built and developed through a relationship of trust with the counsellor; in other cases, with peers. This means counsellors must regularly check for and validate that what has been proposed has been understood, and that they take an interest in their clients' intentions by helping them weigh the pros and cons of their participation;
- Using interpreters or other refugees who have already gone through the process as a model to ensure a full understanding of consent;
- When sensing mistrust, it might be better to have more informal contact through activities that do not require disclosing personal information (e.g., company tours, neighbourhood tours or community support resources). These informal spaces can help gradually create a relationship of trust (Michaud et al., 2012).

It would be unthinkable to address the issue of consent without also discussing issues related to the figure of the counsellor. In the refugee's mind, the supportive role the counsellor plays implicitly confers on them an authority status—someone who knows what is good and who will tell the refugee what needs to be done. Because of this, it is challenging—if not downright impossible in some situations—to have "free and informed consent" in the early stages of counselling. In Québec, consent is inextricably linked to the value of freedom of choice. This value may be vastly different for some refugees, making it difficult at the beginning for some to grasp the meaning of the term. This occurs when refugees test out the right to oppose or question what is being proposed to them, and articulate what they really want or think; this can only occur once they feel confident in the relationship.

Consent thus becomes an ideal activity to introduce the basics of the host culture and the importance of people knowingly consenting to services provided to them as part of a professional relationship.

A First-hand Account from a Career Counsellor

To help refugees understand how helping professions work in Québec, I noticed it is easier for them to understand when you draw parallels with the types of help they are familiar with and stress the differences and similarities. For example, for some refugees, getting help means that the helper, typically a professional, spiritual or elder (life experience) person:

- listens, understands and advises on what to think and/or do;
- takes charge of problems to solve them.

I sometimes find myself referring new immigrants to Canada to newcomer services or healthcare services, Francization services, etc. By naming these different forms of assistance, it is easier to introduce refugees to the specific role of counsellors compared to what they had been familiar with. In fact, I found that it's in the experience of dealing with counsellors that an understanding of informed consent is developed.

The consent form can be used by counsellors to explain about rights, responsibilities and expectations in guidance and SOI, to learn about participant expectations and mediate between their system of reference and the other's. For those refugees who are not fully fluent in the language of the host society, there is a range of translation tools (interpreters, translation software) that can be tapped into.

The questions and reflections that precede the practice of informed consent in a specific intervention context such as that of refugees with little formal education compels us to call on the entire guidance community to engage in dialogue. We believe the time has come to have practitioners and academic partners develop a database of tools to promote free and informed consent, and offer the questions that follow as a starting point:

- In our eagerness to apply and respect rules—perhaps too rigidly, to protect the public— are we not risking the imposition of one cultural vision over others? Would this not be counterproductive for refugees who would automatically answer "yes" without first understanding the meaning of consent?
- Would it not be better to opt for a negotiated meaning, even when this could mean deviating from standard consent forms, a sine qua non tool for public protection in guidance practices?
  - For example, could we not consider translating free and informed consent forms into different languages? Would it not be better if the translated version were presented in multimedia formats other than writing (e.g., audio or video clips) and include tips given by other immigrants?

Following these suggestions, the meaning of this practice could be then adapted to the real needs of refugees and still comply with underlying professional standards.

1.2 Assessment

According to the 2010 *Guide d'évaluation en orientation/ Assessment Guide for Career and Guidance Counselling*. published by the Ordre des conseillers et conseillères d'orientation du Québec [Québec College of Guidance Counsellors, OCCOQ], assessment activities are key components of career and guidance counselling, regardless of the client.

As a starting premise for assessment in an intercultural context, it is important to remember that "all people irrespective of origin, social background, family, education [...] and irrespective of their relationship with the written word, have the ability to learn and that their development is ongoing. Experience is essential to personal development. To be 'developmental,' the experience— which involves the subject—must be processed and the person must give it some meaning" (Mouillet & Barberet, 2005, pp.13-14, free translation).

The second premise is that people's ability to reflect on themselves, their circumstances and the world is not solely dependent on their education or proficiency in reading and writing. In fact, in some societies, people can "think" rigorously in forms of orality strongly rooted in certain social contexts of origin.

As part of their practice, career counsellors "[a]ssess psychological functioning, personal resources and the conditions of the milieu, respond to needs with regard to identity, and develop and maintain proactive adjustment strategies with a view to helping a person make personal and vocational choices throughout life, regain socio-vocational autonomy and carry out career projects in interaction with his environment" (OCCOQ, 2010, p.3).

Assessment is thus structured around three dimensions—psychological functioning, personal resources and environmental conditions. In the case of refugees, however, it seems fitting to add a fourth dimension: cultural identity and acculturation strategies. These four dimensions are detailed in the table below.

Table 22. Assessment Dimensions in Counselling Refugees

Dimension	Indicators About the Individual and their Relationship with Others
Cultural Identity and Acculturation Strategies	• Cultural identity: communities (e.g., social, political, regional, national, ethnic, religious) a person identifies with in terms of values, ideas and commitment, language and living environment, practices, traditions and beliefs, collective experiences and historical memory. • Transitional identity issues. • Links between one's own culture and the host society. • Social isolation or involvement in the host community. • Acculturation strategies. • Relationship to time and context. • Social gender roles. • Relationship to authority. • Relationship to society or collective contribution. • Relationship to family, education and employment.
Psychological Functioning	• State of health during migration and today. • Resilience. • Quality of self-esteem and self-confidence. • Values. • Interests. • Aptitudes. • Strengths or qualities. • Ideas. • Emotions. • Behaviours. • Self-regulation and self-protection methods. • Presence of mental or neuropsychological disorders. • Presence of intellectual disabilities. • Presence of a disability. • Difficulties adapting to the school or the workplace. • Other.

Assessment Dimensions in Counselling Refugees

Dimension	Indicators About the Individual and their Relationship with Others
Personal Resources	• Self-knowledge. • Knowledge of the labour market. • Knowledge of available training. • Knowledge of public institutions in the host country and their administrative requirements. • Knowledge of available services and opportunities in their community. • Skills, informal and formal learning. • Level of education. • Area(s) of expertise. • Specialized skills. • Spoken language(s). • Computer skills. • Competency cards. • State of physical and mental health. • Socio-demographic variables (e.g., age, gender, ethnic background, judicial status, marital status and marital, parental and family obligations). • Financial resources. • Transportation (e.g., driver's licence, access to a car or public transit).
Environmental Conditions	• Immediate or future nuclear or extended family support. • Immigration status (final or pending). • Institutional support to facilitate understanding administrative requirements related to the SOI process in the host society. • Family finances and the urgency of the SOI. • Places where they have ties with family and friends. • Groups or places for educational, job or social activities. • Networking opportunities to access information about available jobs. • Socioeconomic status of people. • Type of job. • Parental level of education. • Access to career guidance services. • Attributes of certain professions. • Labour laws and regulations, etc. • Social, education and labour policies.

Assessing **cultural identity and acculturation strategies** can be done in dialogue with refugees using the notional foundations introduced in Section 2 of Part Three. The goal of assessing this dimension is to determine its possible influence on the career, education or life plans they care about, or think is within their reach. For example, when a refugee adopts a separation or segregation strategy, this can mean refusing to go to school or finding a job that would involve close contact with people from the host society. Once this potential influence has been isolated, it can be discussed in terms of impact on possible career or workplace choices. Similarly, assessing the relationship to social gender roles of participants in a group can help determine the relevance of a discussion about potential discrepancies between these concepts depending on cultural and/or sub-cultural affiliation and possible expectations on the part of HR or co-workers in this regard.

Some assessment indicators—particularly those related to **psychological functioning**—may also be more difficult to identify at first in refugees with little formal education. They are more likely to manifest later in the process, possibly due to the many challenges these refugees face and the reticence to talk about their personal life, which they may not realize the importance of (see Part One). This is a further argument in favour of ongoing assessment.

For specialized guidance professionals, to be able to assess refugees with little formal education in the context of the host society, we suggest assessment should be carried out throughout the counselling and integration process. This should start with what has been actioned by the refugees instead of just in advance of the SOI, all the while keeping in mind the four assessment dimensions. This enables the guidance professional to comprehend how refugees are leveraging **personal resources** (e.g., strategies and skills) developed in their country of origin, and whether they are doing it similarly or differently in the host country. Ongoing assessment allows a focus on other indicators and is important for refugees, who undergo a gradual change as they integrate into the host society and become more familiar with how it works.

While assessing the **environmental conditions** of refugees with little formal education is certainly warranted, it must, in many cases, spur action on the part of counsellors: better describing barriers or knowing about them is simply not enough. Counsellors will likely need to ensure that environmental conditions are aligned with their clients' plans and intentions. They could for example, reach out to businesses to request internships on their behalf or initiate contact with an aid organization and accompany the refugee there. In addition, to ensure a rigorous assessment, they would probably need to gather important information from other support workers (teachers, external counsellors, etc.).

The above details thus have an impact on guidance provided to refugees with little formal education: counsellors need to be attentive to refugees' realities and ensuing needs and consider that, at times, they may need to change the way they are accustomed to working. For example, a plan jointly made with the refugee may change several times; being flexible, adjusting and expecting ups and downs is essential to maintain a relationship of trust. To help counsellors be prepared to anticipate some of these possible changes, the following table lists some practical considerations we feel are important when assessing and supporting refugees with little formal education.

Table 23 : Practical Considerations for Assessing Refugees with Little Formal Education

Practical Considerations for Assessing Refugees with Little Formal Education
• The choice of guidance may be driven by a sense of urgency: to meet family needs, for example (e.g., pay rent, feed kids, pay for daycare).
• The importance a refugee lends to the information provided during meetings can vary considerably depending on their understanding of the counsellor's role and/or opinions of influential external sources (e.g., religious leaders, father, brother).
• The relevance of using psychometric tools needs to be evaluated based on their validity for this target population. To our knowledge, very few of these tools are well suited for refugees with little formal education. That said, the Inventaire visuel d'intérêts professionnels [Visual Career Interests Inventory, IVIP], comprising a list of semi-skilled occupations depicted in images (Dupont et al., 2018), may be a constructive option.
• The sheer volume of information might lead some refugees with little formal education to feel overwhelmed and be unwilling to decide or make a choice; to help them grasp the realities of the labour market, opting for visual information and trying things out can be useful to guide them.
• To avoid retraumatization in assessing these refugees, it is best not to delve into the complex interpersonal traumas they have experienced (see Part One). It is best to let them speak voluntarily when they feel ready. However, it is important to be on the lookout for the needs these traumas can create. For example, in groups, many refugees feel the need to be unconditionally loved and supported by counsellors. At times, it may also be necessary to refer a refugee to specialized resources.

Lastly, as Olry-Louis (2020) points out, counsellors who work with refugees with little formal education would greatly benefit from applying broader assessments than they do with other types of clients. These refugees feel it is important to have a space to be heard and share the pains and emotions they experienced or continue to experience. In these cases, it would be prudent to:

- Reflect with them on their life priorities and the role of work in their lives;
- Discuss expectations laid out so far;
- Identify current limitations to employment;
- Rank the challenges they face and think in terms of goals;
- Be cognizant of the sometimes-significant gap between ways of doing things in the country of origin and applicable standards in the host country.

1.3   Labour Market Information (LMI)

Labour market information (LMI) is defined as "any knowledge, facts, data or forecasts that Canadians can use to make decisions about their learning, education, training, employment and workplace" (CIMT, 2020, free translation). Others define it as information about training and work (Supeno & Mongeau, 2015), including formal, non-formal and informal education. Providing LMI can be a service in its own right or can be folded into counselling or an SOI. This service is found in educational institutions and employment assistance organizations.

Some of the options often considered by refugees with little formal education are semi-skilled or low-skilled trades, vocational training (e.g., Attestation of Vocational Studies in Québec) or work/study programs. Entrepreneurial opportunities can also be explored. In disseminating LMI about possible job options, however, it is important to pay attention to gendered representations of occupations, not least because of the potentially different treatment of social gender roles in the refugee's culture. Group discussions and exchanges might gradually bring some of these refugees to be open to the idea of working in non-traditional occupations (Dionne et al., 2020). As with anyone born in Québec or in Canada, this receptiveness opens the door to a wider range of potential occupations or careers.

Providing information about available recognition of prior learning programs is also part of LMI. The Ministère de l'Éducation, du Loisir et du Sport (2005) has stated that: "The recognition of prior learning and competencies is a process that allows adults to obtain official recognition for competencies in relation to socially established standards, such as those set out in programs of study" (p.5). This recognition is critical for refugees with little formal education, as they may have developed their skills in an informal setting in their country of origin or while migrating. The kind of skills recognized tend to be generic or those related to semi-skilled occupations. In the end, a number of factors need to be considered when passing on LMI to refugees. These are listed in the table below.

Table 24 : Practical Considerations When Providing LMI to Refugees with Little Formal Education.

Practical Considerations When Providing LMI to Refugees with Little Formal Education
• Do not take for granted that LMI given to refugees with little formal education has been understood. It is important to provide timely opportunities for practical application or offer concrete examples of the tasks involved in working in a trade or profession in the host country (e.g., using videos or short-term internships). Like many young adults, refugees (Supeno et al., 2020) prefer to ask for advice about their career guidance or SOI from significant people in their lives. When they get this advice from family or friends, they can be asked to report on and discuss it. The counsellor may then introduce them to other people or sources who can validate this information.

Practical Considerations When Providing LMI to Refugees with Little Formal Education.

- As Savard et al. (2007) point out, LMI is not neutral and can be confusing. It is important to remember that even though providing information is a seemingly technical task, it is also indispensable to look at what these individuals experience in the face of new opportunities or regarding barriers to working in a desired job in the host society.
- Bear in mind that when presenting LMI to a group, it may be confrontational and/or sensitive.
- It is important to assist with the search for information and use technology to do so.
- When presenting information in a classroom, it is best to work in partnership with the SOI teacher, who can prepare the refugees in advance of the workshop.
- Exploring unskilled occupations can be an attractive option for refugees that lets them quickly enter the labour market.

2
Working Alliances in the Career Guidance of Refugees with Little Formal Education

2.1 Working Alliances

Whether in psychology or educational and career guidance, Bordin's definition (1979) of working alliances is generally used. For Bordin, this alliance involves consideration of goals and tasks and the emotional bond built through intervention.[33] The importance of working alliances in the field of guidance and counselling has been well documented (Massoudi et al., 2008; Milot-Lapointe et al., 2021; Perdrix, 2013; Whiston et al., 2016): the stronger the counsellor-client alliance, the greater the satisfaction with the guidance process (Massoudi et al., 2008; Milot-Lapointe et al., 2021). It is also associated with positive outcomes for clients' careers, their mental health and their opinions on the quality of the counsellor's work (Milot-Lapointe et al., 2021).

A working alliance is not only the heart of the guidance process in the context of an individualized counselling; it also holds true for group counselling. In the latter, however, the concept of working alliances gets broadened to encompass 1) The relationship between counsellor and group; 2) The relationship between the participants themselves; and 3) The relationship of a participant or the counsellor with the group (Lo Coco et al., 2022). The working alliance is established at the outset of the intervention process and continues throughout its duration.

The clarity of the goals and tasks proposed, as well as the strength and quality of the counsellor-client relationship, bring their own set of challenges to interventions with refugees with little formal education. It is thus crucial to consider important variables such as proximity to family and the involvement of diverse institutional partners and the workplace, to name but a few. In addition, in the early stages of this relationship, many of these refugees may have trouble articulating their expectations of the process. This will take time but will become clearer along the way. Counsellors therefore need to hone their intercultural intervention skills to fully grasp the realities of the refugees standing in front of them and be open and empathetic to the challenges experienced. The intervention will then undoubtedly be different, as it will require a realignment of the counsellor's and refugee's respective cultural stances.

---

33 Horvath (2001) defines it as a positive emotional bond.

2.2   Building a Strong Working Alliance

2.2.1   With the Person or the Group

Creating an atmosphere that is warm and welcoming makes it easier to build a working alliance. Building this alliance can be done, in fact, through kind gestures such as taking the time to greet participants and showing a real interest in them before getting down to brass tacks. Taking an interest in someone who comes from a country with a predominantly collectivist culture means much more than a perfunctory "Hi, how are you?" It means inquiring about their closely knit circles of family and friends (e.g., uncles and aunts, grandparents, children, spouse).

In the counselling process, welcoming is integral to the relationship, and for refugees with little formal education, it is of prime importance. In addition to their role as advisors, counsellors can be perceived as representatives of the host society. Their warm and empathetic demeanor will indeed show refugees that they are welcome and loved. Showing such a welcome is far from trivial in the eyes of people who have often been victims of violence and rejection. Particular care is needed here. Additionally, counsellors with many years of experience working with refugees find that in group interventions, it is important to make a number of small gestures before people arrive and when greeting them.[34]

Table 25 : Practical Considerations When Greeting Refugees Individually or in a Group

Practical Considerations When Greeting Refugees Individually or in a Group
• Create a welcoming environment with decorative objects evoking the cultural heritage of members of the group.
• Greet them with some tea and an assortment of typical foods (sweets, fruits).
• Greet each member of the group individually with a handshake or a similar gesture, tailored to the person.
• Take the time to inquire about each person in their circle (being aware that they may answer politely by always saying everything is fine).
• Take an interest in the personal history, customs and traditions of each member of the group: life in their country of origin, migration history, ties with the "old country," family and extended family members, current situation (challenges, languages spoken/written, support network, family, state of health, employment history in Québec and country of origin, education in general, what is important in education in their country of origin, what social success means to them, etc.), bereavements, needs, values. These are some of the things you should get them to talk about.
• Let them know at the outset they will be getting a certificate for having achieved the objectives of the support program.

---

34 These strategies can also be applied to one-on-one interventions.

Doing all these small gestures may require a good deal of time and patience on the part of the counsellor. Evidence shows, however, that it is worth the effort, as it establishes a strong trust relationship and working alliance. These gestures should continue throughout the process to ensure the refugees are always welcomed warmly.

As we have seen in Part One, the multiple challenges faced by refugees generate particular hardships and ultimately a loss of privileges (IRESMO, 2017). As denizens of the host society, counsellors need to bear in mind these difficult experiences and accommodate them without necessarily forcing their disclosure. The tasks proposed to refugees as well as their meaning in their career guidance and integration need to be clearly laid out; the same goes for the goal of the process, so as to create an environment conducive to intervention and a strong working alliance.

2.2.2   With the Family of Refugees

In providing guidance support that can spread over weeks or months, counsellors can become resources for both refugees and their families. Family is a focal point, because members value the intergenerational transmission and sharing of knowledge, both in learning the language and becoming familiar with cultural and administrative elements of the host society (Vatz Laaroussi et al., 2012). For this reason, families are often involved in career guidance and integration decisions, and counsellors are therefore likely to meet some members of the family and possibly even forge ties with them. When refugees meet with a counsellor, it is important that the latter pays attention to the family and accepts that they will be involved in the process. This is a good way of maintaining a positive link with the refugee and their environment, but it can also create counselling needs for other members of the family. In such cases, counsellors could refer family members to appropriate resources within the organization or in the community.

2.2.3   With Different Partners

When working with refugees, it is worth remembering that establishing a working alliance with other partners is a key part of the process, since cooperation with them requires creating relationships of trust, clarifying common and respective tasks and agreeing on shared goals. However, challenges may differ depending on the partner: the education community, employment assistance or community-based organizations, business and workplace staff, work integration social enterprises or newcomer services agencies.

The Education Community

Depending on the context of the counselling, working alliances may be internal or involve external partners. Different types of communication challenges may surface given the players involved (e.g., counsellors, teachers, receptionists or administration staff). A working alliance established with each of these key players that leverages their expertise will make it possible to clarify respective roles and mandates and act in partnership for refugees to achieve an explicit and shared goal.

Depending on the path of refugees with little formal education, the Francization team in particular can be a valuable ally for the counsellor. This team has already established a trusted relationship with these refugees; they are fully acquainted with their level of language skills as well as efficient learning and communication strategies. An alliance with this team is a must to address key challenges, particularly those related to education and language skills, which are foundational in SOI. Similarly, as they spend a great deal of time with refugee learners, teachers are often on the front line and are well positioned to pinpoint counselling and LMI needs.

Based on the experiences of counsellors we consulted, this alliance contributes to a deeper assessment of refugee situations, who they are and what they learned, and useful means to better define the intervention process. They might conclude, for example, that one person learns more effectively about job integration by listening to stories or anecdotes, or that another—a single mom—could probably use additional support to balance the different spheres of her life. Counsellors would thus benefit from including certain information from multidisciplinary team meetings in their discussion with refugees. They could also make specific references to what was said or done in French courses. This alliance with the education community promotes not only coherent support, but also helps the refugee to see the connection and complementarity between the actions taken by the different stakeholders working toward their integration.

Community or Employment Assistance Organizations

Different community or employment assistance organizations can be important partners as they can assist refugees in developing marketable job skills or getting services to help them integrate. An alliance with and between these organization also makes for a better-coordinated intervention; it also fosters personalized interaction and a better understanding (on the part of refugees) of the diverse support services available and the interrelationships between them.

When a counsellor or another support worker has to announce the end of services, it is best to have a plan in place with the refugee(s) concerned beforehand to ensure they do not feel abandoned: by showing that support can continue through partnerships with diverse organizations, it will be easier to keep the links unbroken. Cooperation between the different staff in organizations can also help move past first impressions and reach a common understanding of refugee realities and needs. As a matter of fact, it is often the counsellor who is the bearer of "the bad news," such as the refugee not qualifying for a desired program (e.g., vocational or basic training) or the end of training, and this may undermine trust: refugees might feel that a personal decision was behind their plans being "blocked."

Counsellors have noted that that when faced with this institutional impasse, some refugees resort to strategies such as saying different things to different people about their plans, depending on who they are dealing with. They could tell the French teacher, for example, "I want to continue taking French" and the counsellor "I want to work." While such talk may seem inconsistent, one way to interpret would be it through the lens of intercultural competency (see Part 3) and identity strategies.

Lastly, although knowledge of and a good working alliance with available local community services are certainly important throughout the integration process, it is especially critical to turn to them when SOI-related challenges persist after the initial service delivery. This can help create a support network and safety net in situations impacting refugees with little formal education or their families. In these cases, ensuring service continuity will help, for example, maintain support for plans refugees have for their future, getting them to fully participate in the host community, continue receiving support and gradually ease into the labour market.

Business and Workplace Staff

An important part of counselling refugees is partnering with players in the labour market. Company tours and collaborations with employers likely to hire or supervise refugees with little formal education make it easier for refugees to learn about the job market and develop a systemic and cultural understanding of it in the host country. Establishing a network of partners is essential for effectively and concretely exploring options in trades or professions, and more broadly, for opening a gateway to SOI. Because of the barriers encountered along their learning path (Dionne et al., 2022b), refugees with little formal education have not always had access to the necessary resources to fulfill their choice of education and occupation. Similarly, their knowledge of labour realities or pursuing a profession in a new world may need to be reinforced. Consequently, as part of counselling, it may be necessary to give these refugees the opportunity to explore workplaces first-hand from the outset to help them better understand the requirements of certain occupations or professions and boost their chances of connecting with players in industries where they may get hired.

Working with the business community can also be an ideal opportunity to have these players join in a conversation about refugee guidance needs and generate a joint understanding of workforce needs. Following various meetings, refugees may be in a better position to know about job opportunities offered by businesses and associate concrete tasks with specific ways of carrying out a job in the host society. Depending on their plans for a job or for contributing to the community, refugees may also be able to work out what type of occupation or company would interest them.

This type of alliance can also be expanded to ensure refugees can continue to attend French classes in a school service centre while working. The Québec government has different funding programs to incentivize learning French on the job.[1] A company based in Sherbrooke is an inspiring example: it employs several refugees under this incentive partnership to take French lessons during working hours.

---

35   See for instance: www.quebec.ca/entreprises-et-travailleurs-autonomes/francisation.

Work Integration Social Enterprises

Work integration social enterprises are defined as both community-based organizations and social economy enterprises: they combine a social mission of producing goods or services with directly supporting integration. They provide gainful employment for 20 to 36 weeks and training support with their SOI to vulnerable populations facing exclusion from the labour market. Most of these enterprises allow employees to try their hand at different job tasks, where they can get support and guidance and acquire transferable skills and knowledge needed to work in the regular labour market. These types of enterprises are found throughout Québec and Canada in many industries ranging from food to textiles, manufacturing to retail. An alliance with these partners through tours and testing out different job tasks for a few days can effectively expedite transitioning to employment for many people.

Although initiatives such as those provided by work integration social enterprises can be especially helpful for refugees with little formal education, very little experience with paid work and the burden of other challenges are likely to hinder integration into the host society over the short term (see Part One). However, these initiatives still serve as a gateway to allow refugees to become acquainted with labour market needs and increasingly gain confidence in their abilities.

A First-hand Account from a Career Counsellor

As part of my work, I had to oversee refugee internships. One supervisor approached me about wanting to develop a relationship of trust with one of the refugees he had recruited into his company. I suggested that he could start a routine of greeting this person every morning when they got to work and take the time to ask after them (about their family, their health), let them know that he was available should they need anything and wish them a good day. After a few days of doing this, the supervisor confirmed he noticed a visible difference in the refugee, who had begun to engage more openly. Happy with this positive outcome, the supervisor asked me how long he should keep this up and I answered, "as long as that person is important to you."

As a counsellor, I'm convinced it's important to explain to partners what this means and how to relate to refugees, in order to develop a meaningful relationship with them.

Newcomer Services Agencies

It is worth reiterating that administrative procedures are a major hurdle in immigrating and settling in Québec or anywhere else in Canada. For this reason, it is important to create working alliances with a network of partners from the different levels of government and administrative services, and then "walk with" (Michaud et al., 2012) refugees with little formal education in dealing with these organizations to meet their diverse integration needs. An alliance with these partners is instrumental in demystifying and better understanding the respective roles of the various government bodies refugees are bound to interact with as part of the inescapable administrative procedures needed throughout their settlement process.

A First-hand Account from a Guidance Counsellor

It is always best to prioritize integrating into the regular labour market to prevent people getting stuck in a cycle of vulnerability. From this perspective, work integration social enterprises should be considered a complementary resource and not a sustainable solution.

A First-hand Account from a Guidance Counsellor

As part of my work, I regularly accompany refugees to a police station to request proof of no criminal record (police certificate), a Canadian requirement to work in certain places (e.g., retirement homes). Because of past negative interactions or misrepresentations of law enforcement, some of these refugees fear going alone. Going with them reassures them, and also helps to downplay this step while at the same time introducing them to the role and functions of law enforcement in the host society.

Table 26 : Practical Considerations Regarding Law Enforcement

Practical Considerations Regarding Law Enforcement
• Inviting a police representative or a refugee who has gone through a police record check could help refugees understand the meaning of this procedure and the feelings it can trigger.
• Regularly check with refugees to see if they have received new requests for information.
• Creating alliances with partners to share responsibilities allows for continued support when the counsellor's organizational resources do not allow them to accompany the refugee through various steps.
• Many legal matters may exceed the expertise of counsellors; try establishing partnerships with refugee or immigrant rights organizations.

3
A Suggested Approach to the Guidance and SOI of Refugees with Little Formal Education

Many career development practices have been built on foundational concepts applicable primarily to North American or European client populations; not many of these concepts and practices have been adjusted to consider migrant realities. Embedding intercultural knowledge into guidance counselling thus poses the need to revisit theoretical concepts that are taken for granted and models of intervention assumed to be absolute truths, and to develop appropriate assessment tools (Goyer, 2003; 2005). As Arthur (2021) argues, a counsellor has the duty to:

> [...] take a critical look at career theories and models regarding the way in which their underlying principles (e.g., rational and independent decision-making; the structure of equal opportunity; inorance of the discriminatory effects of gender, racial and class biases) are culturally bound (p.26, free translation).

The guidance approach we propose in the following pages is intended to develop among refugees with little formal education the ability to find their bearings as they settle in the host society. This first and foremost implies recognition of the skills developed by these refugees along the way. During the guidance process, we also include learning scenarios to help refugees continue developing their skills and improve their understanding of the labour market in the host society. This is in line with Arthur et al. (2023), who advocate for an approach based on social justice and recognition of the strength of these refugees to support them through their career development.

When it comes to refugees with little formal education, the more standard approach used in individual or group counselling and their SOI needs to be adjusted. These adjustments are elemental to the process of working with this population to encourage dialogue and support refugees' learning about their interests, aptitudes and available occupations. The table below summarizes this adapted approach, which we believe merits being put into practice. In it, we have identified two key areas for action, applicable to both individual and group interventions: 1) Actions with the individual or the group; and 2) Actions in and on the environment (with and on behalf of refugees). Inherent in this approach is the fact that some refugees have never had a formal job, either in their country of origin or in the host society.

Table 27 : An Intercultural Approach to Guidance for Refugees with Little Formal Education in their Social and Occupational Integration (SOI)

Keywords	Actions With the Individual or the Group	Actions in and on the Environment (With and on Behalf of Refugees)
Discovering the Labour Market in Relation to the Self		
Welcome, Alliance, Consent	• Welcome the individual(s). • Establish/create a working alliance by defining the individual's or group's needs. • Explain consent and roles of the various stakeholders (See Part Four, section 1.1). • Take an interest in how guidance works in the country of origin.	• Create a welcoming environment. • Give a warm welcome. • Devote time to getting regular updates from individuals on their family members and other significant people (build an emotional connection). • Build alliances with local organizations to ensure basic needs are met.
	Suggested Intervention Approaches: • See Part Four, sections 1.1 and 2.	
Skills, Strengths, Labour Market	• Help the individual name the knowledge, skills and strengths they developed in their country of origin. • Get the individual to identify and recognize the knowledge they acquired and skills they developed both in formal and informal work settings. • Work on self-perception and awareness of the labour market to make it more accessible.	The counsellor should: • Be well acquainted with different job markets to refer the individual to depending on their job plans. • Organize tours of different workplaces and organizations so individuals can observe different occupations first hand. • Provide hands-on opportunities to experiment with different trades or concrete forms of observation and/or exposure.
	Suggested Intervention Approaches: • Ask questions such as: "How did you get your current/last job?" In cases of no previous job experience, discuss activities (e.g., recreational activities, household chores). Ask them what they did in their country of origin. • Introduce the notions of aptitudes and interests after a job tryout. Identify interests and describe aptitudes for each of the tasks observed by the refugee. • Toggle back and forth between the characteristics of the job and what the individual likes (interests), finds important (values) and their priorities: type of industry, duties, short, medium- or long-term work and placement rates.	

An Intercultural Approach to Guidance for Refugees with Little Formal Education in their Social and Occupational Integration (SOI)

Keywords	Actions With the Individual or the Group	Actions in and on the Environment (With and on Behalf of Refugees)
Skills, Strengths, Labour Market	• Following tours, ask for feedback on differences and similarities with the country of origin, what they liked or disliked, etc. • Propose activities where group members give each other feedback on aptitudes or name the aptitudes they see in each other. • Encourage refugees to help each other expand their vocabulary and allow them to say what they like and what they are able to do. • Rate their level of interest for each of the tasks by assigning smiley emojis, other meaningful and concrete symbols, or a colour. • Invite individuals to visually explore as many occupations as possible—through videos, tours, one-day internships—to help represent jobs that match their skill levels and the places they would like to visit. This gets them quickly involved in making choices. • Propose an exercise to gather ideas from people in the refugee circle on possible job options. Give feedback on the exercise by helping each member of the group identify the values that guided them and their family in their choice.	
Assessing and Acting on Environmental Conditions	• Conduct assessments that consider identity and acculturation strategies. • Understand the refugee's worldviews and guidance and integration needs.	• Build bridges with supervisors/ HR managers or mentors to facilitate access to one-day internships or employment. • Connect with mentors and training centres for participating in internships or "student for a day" programs. • Prepare refugees to recognize microaggressions and/or racism. Recommend strategies for dealing with this.

Suggested Intervention Approaches:
• See Part 4, section 1.2.
• Help connect the dots between the culture of origin and that of the host society by showing similarities and differences in guidance and job searches.
• Ask questions about working conditions: What were the working conditions in the job or what are the desired working conditions?
• Ask each member of the group to think about the job requirements of an occupation and name the conditions that are the most important for them and their family.
• Maintain a good relationship with supervisors or HR managers in partner companies to be kept abreast of their needs. This helps refugees concretely explore jobs and optimally match their needs with those of employers.

| **Learning and Meaning of Guidance** | • Seize opportunities to systematically use the same vocational concepts (e.g., unskilled and semi-skilled trades, values) using plain language and help refugees understand them.

• Explain the meaning of current, common terms used in the host society.

• Clarify the different decision-making processes related to guidance and the key people involved. | • Create conducive learning conditions in the different spheres of the refugee's integration (e.g., community, groups, workplace), providing intercultural mediation where needed.

• Foster mutual help in the community (e.g., intergenerational exchange, sponsorships to boost opportunities for practising French). |

Suggested Intervention Approaches:

• Assess activities and job explorations carried out and validate what has been learned.

• Help refugees understand the job market. As they gradually begin to mention their preferences, it will be possible to link the job market with what they know about themselves.

• Take note of those who might be feeling anxious at the thought of having to name their interests or aptitudes; it is sometimes difficult for them to recognize them on their own. We recommend that interests be approached from an educational angle, where the counsellor slowly incorporates through exercises the notion of having liked or liking to do something.

• Seize opportunities to validate skills revealed through various situations and provide feedback. The more the individual can recognize their aptitudes, the more likely they are to develop their sense of self-efficacy.

• Help refugees discover employment contexts that will enable them to make better informed decisions.

Integrating Information About the Self and the Environment

| **Adoption, Communication, Mediation** | • Review exposure to trades, professions and training.

• Use this to clarify the individual's values, interests and aptitudes. | • Play the role of intercultural mediator with relevant players in clarifying the needs of the refugee and those of companies or training centres. |
| **Intentions and Conditions for Application** | • Clarify training or job options refugees wish to pursue for themselves and their family (short-, medium-, or long-term) while bearing in mind urgency and learning potential. | • Support administrative procedures to obtain the necessary documents for being hired and advise about eligibility for a given employment program and/or family support (see Approaches for Counsellors in Part One). |

An Intercultural Approach to Guidance for Refugees with Little Formal Education in their Social and Occupational Integration (SOI)

Keywords	Actions With the Individual or the Group	Actions in and on the Environment (with and on Behalf of Refugees)
Intentions and Conditions for Application	**Suggested Intervention Approaches:** • Encourage establishing links between the job market and what refugees know about themselves, as the latter gradually begin to articulate their preferences. • Help them prioritize the characteristics they discover about themselves and those of the job market so that they can gradually confirm their choice of trade or occupation. A visual tool (e.g., a photo, image or video) can be handy here. • Enable refugees to better understand labour market requirements and get a clearer picture of themselves as employees. • Equip individuals to help better understand their environment. Carry out role-playing exercises on interactions that may create confusion or conflict in the workplace. This allows refugees to experience these situations in a safe environment and get feedback on interaction with co-workers and people in a position of authority. • Talk about experiences in and discoveries made about the workplace environment so the whole group can benefit from them. • Ask them what they learned during the internship or other job exploration activities, what they liked best or least (to help them recognize their interests) and about comments from their co-workers or employer (to encourage them to name their aptitudes).	
	Deciding on and Carrying out Actions	
Planning, Enabling Conditions	• Establish a skills development or action plan. • Evaluate the plan's viability in terms of any potential risk for refugees and their families.	• Ensure conditions are in place to carry out the plan. • Confirm the financial support (e.g., wage subsidies) that employers are eligible to receive to help refugees. . • Act as an advocate* in cases of inequity faced by the refugee. *This role can be carried out throughout the support process.
	Suggested Intervention Approaches: • Get each member of the group to visualize short, medium- and long-term prospects based on their abilities, and help them identify concrete means available to them to keep their hope alive in fulfilling their dreams. This will make decisions easier. • Focus on short-term goals with those who struggle envisioning a long-term perspective. • Help refugees integrate, be motivated, recognize what they can do and have confidence in the future.	

An Intercultural Approach to Guidance for Refugees with Little Formal Education in their Social and Occupational Integration (SOI)

Keywords	Actions With the Individual or the Group	Actions in and on the Environment (with and on Behalf of Refugees)
Planning, Enabling Conditions	• Explain that future prospects do not necessarily have to be only work-related; there are other kinds: material (buying a home, a car, etc.), educational (being able to pay for their children's education); relational (visiting or receiving family from the country of origin, sponsoring someone, etc.). • Develop involvement in the decision-making process to ensure refugees can expand their independence and self-confidence.	
Employment Integration	• Support refugees, in consultation with company supervisors or HR, through the steps of implementing an agreed-upon plan (e.g., job integration or the start of training); continue to be available to address any needs that may surface during the integration. **Suggested Intervention Approaches:** • Encourage refugees to contact their counsellor when their SOI is at risk and they need support. • Keep in mind that the intervention and the relationship with the counsellor are essential to keep up with the plan, since the relational links can make it easier for refugees to contact their counsellor in case of need. • Be available as a counsellor to help cope with the highs and lows of integrating into the host society. Refugees can reach out to their counsellor before taking any decisions or actions, or simply to understand something better. • Mediate with supervisors of new hires to explain about the cultural differences and specific needs of the latter; in other words, raise awareness among company staff.	
Social Engagement and Transformation	• Invite refugees to get involved in promoting guidance and employment services to their family and in their community. • Encourage them to become ambassadors to help their peers access guidance services. • Encourage companies to promote the added value of hiring refugees and recognizing their skills. • Consolidate alliances with local organizations to support job retention. **Suggested Intervention Approaches:** • Invite refugees who have successfully integrated to participate and share their success stories with newly arrived refugees. • Urge companies to spread the word about their experience and encourage other businesses to employ refugees. • Network with various community organizations that provide a range of services (e.g., food banks, thrift stores, Maisons de la famille) to be able to refer refugees to services aligned with their needs.	

In sum, the intercultural approach to guidance intervention proposed in Part Four methodically addresses the complex and diverse realities of refugees with little formal education. It draws not only on the experiences of career counsellors, but also on evidence and theoretical foundations we feel are particularly well-suited in providing counselling and SOI support to this client group. In the following table, Richard et al. (2020) best sum up some of the principles our team embraces in this regard:

Table 28 : Principles for Practical Consideration in Guidance Intervention

Principles for Practical Consideration in Guidance Intervention
• Counsellors who ask questions about the migration history and experiences of a refugee show they care for the whole person, and this will have an impact on their working alliance.   • Refugees are the best experts of their own experience, and this will be valued by the fact counsellors are curious to learn more about their culture, customs, country of origin, etc.   • The migration journey of refugees is marked by many gruelling and traumatic events; this underscores their resilience, courage and resourcefulness and is replete with strategies that can be leveraged in interventions.   • Being empathetic to the refugee's experience (e.g., losses, grief, forced contexts, trauma) is instrumental in gaining a better understanding and undertaking a more robust needs analysis.   • Developing one's intercultural competency and awareness of personal biases helps provide a better-fitting intervention.   • Bear in mind you do not need to know everything—it is best not to "open a Pandora's box."   • Work as a team.   • Follow and respect the pace of refugees as they adapt to their host society, and strive for integration and the development of a social network rather than autonomy at all costs.

Conclusion

The reflections and experiences shared in this guide have made it possible to highlight not only the challenges faced by refugees with little formal education, but also those of people working to support their settlement and easing into the job market of the host society. On the one hand, language, physical and mental health, precarity, learning new social codes, communication, employability and access to resources in the host society all represent considerable barriers that make the social and occupational integration of this group a daunting one. On the other, counsellors need to be aware of the specificities of intervention in an intercultural context to be adequately prepared for the cultural differences underlying relationships with authority, social gender roles, time and context.

The highly complex nature of the SOI of refugees with little formal education represents a major roadblock in the pre- and in-service training of career counsellors, due to a lack of scholarship specifically on the difficulties related to the delivery of guidance to this group. To respond to the legitimate concerns of career counsellors who work with these clients, our team offers—as an attempt to fill these gaps—this resource guide highlighting diverse approaches informed by experiential knowledge and promoting the adoption of a stance based on the development of essential attitudes and intercultural competency. In particular, to support revising practices, especially those relating to the career guidance process, we have also proposed a comprehensive approach aimed at adapting this process to the realities of refugees with little formal education.

The writing done for this guide is but the first chapter of a much longer work; the scholarship herein should be continued by all who are dedicated to supporting this population, be it personally, professionally or politically

Bibliography

Abkhezr, P. and McMahon, M. (2017). Narrative Career Counselling for People with Refugee Backgrounds. International Journal for the Advancement of Counselling, 39(2), 99-111. doi. org/10.1007/s10447-017-9285-z

Agodzo, D. (2014). *Six Approaches to Understanding National Cultures: An Overview of Hofstede's Dimensional Paradigm*. Spring Arbor University. doi.org/10.13140/RG.2.1.5041.8009

Albaret, C. (2020, July 31). *Les signes cachés du stress post-traumatique.* [Video.] YouTube. **https://www.youtube.com/watch?v=JCFM8QUWbeQ**

American Psychological Association (APA). (2017). Multicultural Guidelines: An Ecological Approach to Context, Identity, and Intersectionality. **http://www.apa.org/about/policy/multicultural-guidelines.pdf**

American Psychological Association (APA). (n.d.). Trauma. **www.apa.org/topics/trauma**

Amin, A. (2012). Stratégies identitaires et stratégies d'acculturation : deux modèles complémentaires. *Alterstice*, 2(2). 103-116. **doi.org/10.7202/1077569ar**

Anderson, M.-L., Goodman, J. and Schlossberg, N.K. (2012). *Counseling Adults in Transition: Linking Schlossberg's Theory with Practice in a Diverse World*. Springer Publishing Company. **https://scholarworks.wmich.edu/books/15/**

Arseneault, S. (2020). Mieux comprendre l'accueil des réfugiés pris en charge par l'État dans les régions du Québec à travers le regard des intervenants qui les accompagnent. *Ediqscope*, (14).

Arsenault, S. (2021). L'accueil des réfugiés pris en charge par l'État dans les régions du Québec. *Études ethniques au Canada*, 53(2). 1-21.

Arthur, N. (2014). Social justice and career guidance in the age of talent. *International journal for educational and vocational guidance*, 14(3), 47-60. **doi.org/10.1007/s10775-013-9255-x**

Arthur, N. (2017). Constructivist Approaches to Career Counseling: A Culture-infused Approach. In M. McMahon (Ed.), *Career Counseling: Constructivist Approaches* (2nd Ed.) (pp. 54-64). Routledge.

Arthur, N. (2021). Orientation professionnelle axée sur la culture : lier la culture et la justice sociale aux pratiques relatives à la carrière. In A. Arthur, R. Borgen and M. McMahon, M. (Eds.). *Théories et modèles orientés sur la carrière : des idées pour la pratique (pp.25-38). CERIC.*

Arthur, N. and Collins, S. (2014). Counsellors, Counselling, and Social Justice: The Professional is Political. *Canadian Journal of Counselling and Psychotherapy, 48(3), 171-177.*
https://cjc-rcc.ucalgary.ca/article/view/61030/46310

Arthur, N. and Collins, S. (2017). Culture-infused Counsellor Supervision. In N. Pelling, A. Moir-Bussy, & P. Armstrong (Eds.), The Practice of Clinical Supervision (2nd Ed.). (pp.267-295). Australian Academic Press.

Arthur, N. et Januszkowski, T. (2001). The multicultural counselling competencies of canadian counsellors. *Canadian journal of counselling*, 35(1), 36-48.

Arthur, N., McMahon, M., Abkherz, P. et Woodend, J. (2023). Beyond job placement careers for refugees. *International Journal of Educational and Vocational Guidance.*
https://doi.org/10.1007/s10775-023-09579-x

Association canadienne pour la santé mentale. (2003). *Le coffre à outils.*
https://santementaleca.com/docs/cnsm/03_coffre_outils.pdf

Bajoit, G. (1999). Notes sur la construction de l'identité personnelle. *Recherches sociologiques*, 30, 69-84.

Beaulieu, C. (2019). *L'exclusion sociale vécue par des réfugiés de l'Afrique subsaharienne à Québec et les effets sur leurs conditions de vie et leur santé* [Mémoire, Université Laval].

Béji, K. et Pellerin, A. (2010). Intégration socioprofessionnelle des immigrants récents au Québec : le rôle de l'information et des réseaux sociaux. *Relations industrielles / Industrial Relations*, 65(4), 562–583.
https://doi.org/10.7202/045586ar

Bélisle, R. et Bourdon, S. (dir.) (2015). *Tous ces chemins qui mènent à un premier diplôme. Orientation des adultes sans diplôme dans une perspective d'apprentissage tout au long de la vie.* Rapport de recherche préparé dans le cadre d'une Action concertée MELS, MESS et FRQSC. Centre d'études et de recherches sur les transitions et l'apprentissage (CÉRTA) et Fonds de recherche du Québec – Société et culture (FRQSC).

Benoit, M. et Rondeau, L. (2022). *Intervenir auprès de personnes réfugiées ayant vécu de la violence : le groupe comme espace transculturel.* Ordre des psychologues du Québec. Consulté le 12 juin 2023 sur
https://www.ordrepsy.qc.ca/-/intervenir-personnes-refugiees-groupe-espace-transculturel

Berry, J.W. (2000). Acculturation et identité. Dans J. Costa-Lascoux, M. A. Hily et G. Vermès (Eds.), *Pluralité des cultures et dynamiques identitaires : Hommage à Carmel Camilleri* (p. 81-94). L'Harmattan

Berry, J.W. (2001). A psychology of Immigration. *Journal of social issues*, 57(3), 615-631. doi.org/10.1111/0022-4537.00231

Berry, J.W. et Hou, F. (2021) Immigrant acculturation and wellbeing across generations and settlement contexts in Canada. , *International Review of Psychiatry*, 33(1-2), 140-153, DOI : 10.1080/09540261.2020.1750801

Berry, J.W. et Sam, D. (1997). Acculturation and adaptation. Dans J. W., Berry, M. H. Segall et Ç. Kagitçibasi (Eds), *Handbook of cross-cultural psychology (vol. 3)* (p. 291-326). Allyn et Bacon.

Besson, D. et Valitova, A. (2021). Relations interpersonnelles versus facteurs culturels. Cadre théorique et comparaison de l'impact des valeurs culturelles dans trois cas de conflits en France, Canada et Russie. *Management international / International Management / Gestiòn Internacional*, 25(5), 18–36. https://doi.org/10.7202/1085036ar

Bigras, N., Godbout, N., Hébert, M., Runtz, M., et Daspe, M.-È. (2015). Identity and Relatedness as Mediators between Child Emotional Abuse and Adult Dyadic Adjustment in Women. *Child Abuse et Neglect*, 50(déc), 85-93. https://doi.org/10.1016/j.chiabu.2015.07.009

Bilge, S. (2010). De l'analogie à l'articulation : théoriser la différentiation sociale et l'inégalité complexe. *L'Homme et la société*, 2-3(176-177), 43-64. doi.org/10.3917/lhs.176.0043

Bimrose, J. et McNair, S. (2011). Career support for migrants: transformation or adaptation? *Journal of vocational behavior*, 78(2011) 325-333. Doi: 10.1016/j.jvb.2011.03.012.

Bordin, E. S. (1979). The generalizability of the psychoanalytic concept of the working alliance. *Psychotherapy: Theorie, research and practice*, 16(3), 252-260.

Bronfenbrenner, U. (1976). The experimental ecology of education. *Educational Researcher*, 5(9), 5-15. doi.org/10.3102/0013189X005009005

Bronfenbrenner U. (1979). *The ecology of human development: Experiments by nature and design*. Harvard University Press.

Bronfenbrenner U. (2004). *Making human being human. Bioecological perspectives on human development*. Sage Publications

Brown, D. (2007). *Career information, career counseling, and career development* (9th Ed.). Allyn & Bacon.

Brunel, M.-L. (1989). L'empathie en counseling interculturel. *Santé mentale au Québec*, 14(1), 81–94. https://doi.org/10.7202/031490ar.

Camilleri, C. (1990). Identité et gestion de la disparité culturelle : Essai d'une typologie. In C. Camilleri, J. Kastersztein, E. Lipianski, H. Malewska-Peyre, I. Taboada-Léonetti et A. Vasquez (dir.), *Stratégies identitaires* (p. 85-110). PUF.

Camilleri, C. (1990). *Stratégies identitaires*. PUF.

Castro Zavala, S. (2013). Politiques d'immigration: femmes et violence conjugale dans le contexte québécois. *Violence conjugale et diversité culturelle, 3*(2) 97-109. **https://doi.org/10.7202/1077524ar**

Cedefop (2014). *Valuing diversity: guidance for labour market integration of migrants.* Publications Office of the European Union. Cedefop working paper; No 24. Publications Office of the European Union.

Clayton, P. (2006). Blank slates or hidden treasure? Assessing and building on the experiential learning of migrant and refugee women in European countries. *International Journal of Lifelong Education, 24*(3), 227-242. Doi: 10.1080/02601370500134917

Clerc, I. (2019). Quelles règles d'écriture se donner pour communiquer avec l'ensemble des citoyens du Québec ?. *Éla. Études de linguistique appliquée,* 195, 305-324. **https://doi.org/10.3917/ela.195.0305**

Cohen-Émérique, M. (1993). L'approche interculturelle dans le processus d'aide. *Santé mentale au Québec, 18*(1), 71-91. **https://doi.org/10.7202/032248ar**

Cohen Emerique, M. (2007). *L'approccio Interculturale nel Lavoro con gli Immigrati* [The Intercultural Approach in Working with Migrants]. In M. Santerini and P. Reggio (Eds.), Formazione interculturale: teoria e pratica. Milan: Edizioni Unicopli. **www.cohen-emerique.fr/medias/files/cohen-emerique-2007-chapitre-l-approche-interculturelle-aipres-migrants.pdf.**

Cohen-Émerique, M. (2013). Étude des pratiques des travailleurs sociaux en situations interculturelles : Une alternance entre recherches théoriques et pratiques de formation. In Association française pour le développement de la recherche en travail social (Ed.), *Quels modèles de recherche scientifique en Travail Social?* (pp. 233-260). Presses de l'EHESP.

Cohen-Emerique, M. (2015). Chapitre 6 : Les ethnocentrismes et leurs origines : enculturation, socialisation et professionnalisation. In M. Cohen-Emerique (Ed.), *Pour une approche interculturelle en travail social : Théories et pratiques* (pp. 103-122). Presses de l'EHESP.

Collin-Vézina, D. (2016). *Enfants et adolescents victimes de multiples traumatismes : comprendre la problématique pour mieux intervenir. [Training module.]* Formation Porte-Voix. Centre de recherche sur l'enfance et la famille.

Conseil canadien pour les réfugiés / Canadian Council for Refugees (CCR). (2023). Information de base sur les réfugiés. **https://ccrweb.ca/fr/information-base-sur-refugies**

Conseil de l'information sur le marché du travail (CIMT). (2020, February 20). Qu'est-ce que l'IMT. [Video]. YouTube. **https://www.youtube.com/watch?v=8f-pEu1sPJwett=2s**

Conseil supérieur de l'éducation (CSE). (2021). *L'inclusion des familles immigrantes :* pour une synergie accrue en éducation des adultes. Le Conseil. **https://www.cse.gouv.qc.ca/publications/inclusion-familles-immigrantes-50-0542/**

Delory-Momberger, C. and Mbiatong, J. (2011). Nouvelles pratiques d'accompagnement dans les chantiers d'insertion et co-construction des savoirs d'action entre praticiens et chercheurs. *L'Orientation scolaire et professionnelle,* 40(4) [en ligne] **https://doi.org/10.4000/osp.** 3628

Dezutter, O., Babin, J. and Lépine, M. (2018). *Des communautés engagées pour la littératie.* Collectif CLÉ.

Dionne, P., Dupuis, A. et Saussez, F. (2022a). Intégration sociale et professionnelle de personnes réfugiées : la fonction des instruments conceptuels transmis dans un groupe de counseling de carrière. *Diversité urbaine.*

Dionne, P. Joncas, J-A. et Charrette, J. (2022b). ratiques de soutien au cours d'un groupe d'intégration sociale et professionnelle : retombées sur les capabilités de personnes réfugiées dans leur parcours d'apprentissages. *Nouveaux Cahiers de la recherche en éducation,* 24(1), 87-110. **https://doi.org/10.7202/1095696ar**

Dionne, P., Simard, A., Bourdon, S., Supeno, E. et Girardin, V. (2020a). *Guide d'animation de groupes d'orientation S'Orienter.* Sherbrooke: Centre d'études et de recherches sur les transitions et l'apprentissage (CÉRTA)

Doray, P., Lépine, A. Bilodeau, J. (2020). L'orientation scolaire sous l'emprise des rapports sociaux de sexe. La situation de l'enseignement postsecondaire au Québec.. *L'orientation scolaire et professionnelle,* 49(2), 225-256. **https://doi.org/10.4000/osp.** 11962

Dubé, E. (2014). *Réseaux sociaux chez les réfugiés bhoutanais à Québec.* Une question de langue et de malentendus interculturels [Dissertation.] Université Laval

Dupont, P., Gingras, M. et Tétreau, B. (2018). *Inventaire visuel d'intérêts professionnels (IVIP).* Société GRICS.

El-Awad, U., Fathi, A., Lohaus, A. Petermann, F. and Reinelt, T. (2022). Different Relations of Religion and Mental Health. *European Journal of Health Psychology,* 29(1), 26-37. **https://doi.org/10.1027/2512-8442/a000100**

Fleury, C. and Luc, S. (2022). Insertion socio-économique de jeunes Québécois admis au Canada durant l'enfance en tant que réfugiés. *Hommes et Migrations, janvier-mars* 2022(1336), 43-52. **doi.org/10.4000/hommesmigrations.13573**

Flores, L.Y. (2009). Empowering life choice: career counseling in the context of race and class. Dans N.C. Gysbers, M.J., Heppner et J.A. Johnston (dir.) (p. 49-74), *Career counseling : contexts, processes and techniques*. Allyn & Bacon.

Fouad, N.A. et Bryars-Winston, A. M. (2005). ultural Context of Career Choice: Meta-Analysis of Race/ Ethnicity Differences. *The Career Development Quarterly*, 53(3),
223-233. doi.org/10.1002/j.2161-0045.2005.tb00992.x

Frounfelker, R.L., Mishra, T., Carroll, A., Brennan, R.T., Gautam, B., Abdullahi Alas Ali, E. and Betancourt, T.S. (2021). Past trauma, resettlement stress, and mental health of older Bhutanese with a refugee life experience. *Aging & Mental health*, 26(11),
2149-2158. **doi.org/10.1080/13607863.2021.1963947**

Gagné P.P., Leblanc, N., Rousseau A. and Lussier, F. (2009). *Apprendre... une question de stratégies* : développer les habiletés liées aux fonctions exécutives. *Chenelière éducation*.

Gibbons, M.M., Brown, E.C., Daniels, S., Rosecrance, P., Hardin, E.E. and Farrell, I. (2019). Building on Strengths While Addressing Barriers: Career Interventions in Rural Appalachian Communities. *Journal of career development*, 46(6), 637-650.
doi.org/10.1177/0894845319827652

Giguère, É., St-Arnaud, L., Bilodeau, K. (2020). Travail invisible et rapports sociaux de sexe lors des parcours d'insertion socioprofessionnelle des femmes cadres. *L'orientation scolaire et professionnelle*, 49 (2), 281-312.
doi.org/10.4000/osp.1207

Godbout, N., Milot, T., Collin-Vézina, D., and Girard, M. (2018). Répercussions liées au traumas complexes. In T. Milot, N. Godbout, and D. Collin-Vézina. (Eds.), *Le trauma complexe: Comprendre, évaluer et intervenir* (pp.75-95). Presses de l'Université du Québec.

Gonzalez, J., Barden, S. M. et Sharp, J. (2018). Multicultural competence and the working alliance as predictors of client outcomes. *The professional counselor*, 8(4), 314-327. Doi: 10.15241/jg.8.4.314

Goyer, L. (2003). *Dynamiques interculturelles en espace carriérologique : défis posés à la profession des conseillères et conseillers en orientation*. [Doctoral dissertation, UQÀM].

Goyer, L. (2005). Intervenir en situation interculturelle : exigences multipliées en orientation. En pratique, 3, 12-14.

Goyer, L. (in press). *Processus d'intervention en orientation et situations interculturelles*. Québec: ADACO.

rochtdreis, T., König, H-H., Riedel-Heller, S.G. and Dams, J. (2022). Health-Related Quality of Life of Asylum Seekers and Refugees in Germany: A Cross-Sectional Study with Data from the German Socio-Economic Panel. *Applied Research in Quality Life* 17, 109–127. doi.org/10.1007/s11482-020-09877-4

Guay-Charrette, A. (2010). *L'accès au logement par les nouveaux arrivants à Montréal : le cas des réfugiés et demandeurs d'asile en provenance d'Afrique subsaharienne* [Dissertation.] Université du Québec à Montréal.

Guichard, J. and Huteau, M. (2005). *Orientation et insertion professionnelle. Dunod.*

Guichard, J. and Huteau, M. (2007). *Orientation et insertion professionnelle. 75 concepts clés.* Dunod.

Hall, E.T. (1976). Beyond Culture. Doubleday.

Hall, E.T. (1984). Monochronic and Polychronic Time. *In The Dance of Life: The Other Dimension of Time* (pp. 44–58). Anchor Press/Doubleday.

Hall, E.T. (1987). *Au-delà de la culture.* (M.-H. Hatchuel, Trans.) Éditions du Seuil. (Original work published 1976)

Hall, E.T., Hall, M.R. (1990), *Understanding cultural differences – Germans, French and Americans.* Intercultural Pres.

Hall, E.T., Petita A. and Fabre-Luce, A. (2014). *La dimension cachée* (Ser. Points. Essais, 89). Éditions Points.

Hanley, J., Mhamied, A.A., Cleveland, J., Hajjar, O., Hassan, G., Ives, N., Khyar, R. and Hynie, M. (2018). The Social Networks, Social Support and Social Capital of Syrian Refugees Privately Sponsored to Settle in Montreal: Indications for Employment and Housing During their Early Experiences of Integration. Canadian Ethnic Studies, 50(2), 123-148. **doi.org/10.1353/ces.2018.0018**

Hattie, J. (2017). *L'apprentissage visible pour les enseignants : Connaître son impact pour maximiser le rendement des élèves* (Éducation-intervention No 43). Presses de l'Université du Québec.

Hofstede, G. (1994). The business of international business is culture. *International Business Review, 3*(1), 1-14. **doi.org/10.1016/0969-5931(94)90011-6**

Hofstede, G. (2011). Dimensionalizing Cultures: The Hofstede Model in Context. *Online Readings in Psychology and Culture, 2*(1). **doi.org/10.9707/2307-0919.1014**

Hofstede, G., Hofstede, G.J. and Minkov, M., (2010). *Cultures and Organizations: Software of the Mind* (3rd Ed.). McGraw-Hill Professional.

Horvath, A. O. (2001). The Alliance. *Psychotherapy, 38*(4), 365-372.
doi.org/10.1037/0033-3204.38.4.365

Houdé, O. (2014). *Le raisonnement.* Presses Universitaires de France

Institut de recherche et éducation sur les mouvements sociaux (IRESMO). (2017). Oppositions à l'intersectionnalité : malentendus ou résistances ? *Revue De(s)générations, 28,* 7-23.

Joly, M.-P. (2019). The Employment and Occupational Status of Migrants from Countries Experiencing Armed Conflict. *Journal of international migration and integration,* (20), 1071-1095.
https//doi.org/10.1007/s12134-018-00642-z

Kilani, M. (2014). Chapitre 14. L'ethnocentrisme du discours anthropologique. Pour un universalisme critique. In M. Kilani (Ed.), *Pour un universalisme critique : Essai d'anthropologie du contemporain* (pp. 286-295). La Découverte.

Kirmayer, L. J. (2002). *Le dilemme du réfugié. L'évolution Psychiatrique, 67*(4), 743–763.
https://doi.org/10.1016/S0014-3855(02)00167-6

Krammer, S., Kleim, B., Simmen-Janevska, K., and Maercker, A. (2016). Childhood trauma and complex posttraumatic stress disorder symptoms in older adults: A study of direct effects and social-interpersonal factors as potential mediators. *Journal of Trauma & Dissociation, 17*(5), 593–607.
doi.org/10.1080/15299732.2014.991861

Laberge, C. (2020). *Effets d'une séquence de prise de conscience des processus d'écoute menée auprès de personnes peu scolarisées ou peu alphabétisées apprenant le français.* [Master's Dissertation.] Université Laval.

L'Agence des Nations Unies pour les réfugiés / UN Refugee Agency (UNHCR). (2023). Asile et migration.
https://www.unhcr.org/fr/asile-et-migration.html

amar, M.R., Forbes, L. K., and Capasso, L.A. (2019). Helping Working Mothers Face the Challenges of an Intensive Mothering Culture. *Journal of mental health counseling, 4*(3), 203-220.
doi.org/10.17744/mehc.41.3.02

Lambert, E. (2014). *La régionalisation de l'immigration : le cas des réfugiés colombiens installés dans les régions du Québec* [Dissertation.] Université du Québec à Montréal.

Lavoie, N., Lévesque, J.-Y. and Aubin-Horth, S. (2008). Le retour en formation chez les adultes peu scolarisés : un faisceau d'obstacle. *Éducation et sociétés, 2*(22), 161-178. Doi : 10.3917/es.022.0161.

Lazarus, R. S. and Folkman, S. (1984). *Stress, appraisal and coping*. Spiringer Publishing Company.

Le Bossé, Y. (2016). *Soutenir sans prescrire*. Éditions ARDIS.

Lin, S., Kobayashi, K., Tong, H., Davison, K.M., Arora, S.R.A. and Fuller-Thomson, E. (2020). Close Relations Matter: The Association Between Depression and Refugee Status in the Canadian Longitudinal Study on Aging (CLSA). *Journal of immigrant and Minority Health, 22(12), 946-956.* **Doi: 10.1007/s10903-020-00980-0**

Lo Coco, G., Gullo, S., Albano, G., Brugnera, A., Flückiger, C., and Tasca, G. A. (2022). The alliance-outcome association in group interventions: A multilevel meta-analysis. *Journal of Consulting and Clinical Psychology, 90(6),* 513–527. **https://doi.org/10.1037/ccp0000735**

Ma, C. (2022). Ethnocentrisme. In *L'Encyclopédie Canadienne / The Canadian Encyclopedia.* **www.thecanadianencyclopedia.ca/fr/article/ethnocentrisme**

Marchioni, R. (2016). La réunification familiale : un enjeu essentiel. *Droits et libertés, 35*(1), p. 21-25.

Massengale, M., Shebuski, K.M., Karaga, S., Choe, E., Hong, J., Hunter, T.L. and Dispenza, F. (2020). Psychology of Working Theory With Refugee Persons: Applications for Career Counseling. *Journal of career development, 47*(5), 562-605. Doi: 10.1177/0894845319832670.

Massoudi, K., Masdonati, J., Clot-Siegrist, E., Franz, S., and Rossier, J. (2008). Évaluation des effets du counseling d'orientation : influence de l'alliance de travail et des caractéristiques individuelles. *Pratiques Psychologiques, 14*(2), 117-136. **https://doi.org/10.1016/j.prps.2007.11.010**

May, P. (2022). Le Canada : pays de « l'immigration choisie » ? *Hommes et Migrations, janvier-mars* 2022(1336), 196-203.

Michaud, G. (2003). *Étude du transfert des apprentissages dans le cadre des démarches de counseling d'orientation.* Doctoral Thesis.] Université de Sherbrooke. **https://savoirs.usherbrooke.ca/handle/11143/911**

Michaud, G., Bélisle, R., Garon, S., Bourdon, S. and Dionne, P. (2012). *Développement d'une approche visant à mobiliser la clientèle dite éloignée du marché du travail.* Rapport final de la recherche déposé au Ministère de l'Emploi et de la Solidarité sociale. Sherbrooke : Centre d'études et de recherches sur les transitions et l'apprentissage (CÉRTA).

Milot-Lapointe, F., Le Corff, Y. and Arifoulline, N. (2021). A Meta-Analytic Investigation of the Association Between Working Alliance and Outcomes of Individual Career Counseling. *Journal of career assessment, 29*(3), 486-501. Doi: 10.1177/1069072720985037

Ministère de l'Éducation, du Loisir et du Sport (MELS). (2005). *econnaissance des acquis et des compétences en formation professionnelle et technique. Cadre général – Cadre technique / Recognition of Prior Learning and Competencies in Vocational and Technical Training: General and Technical Frameworks.* Gouvernement du Québec. https://cdn-contenu.quebec.ca/cdn-contenu/adm/min/education/publications-adm/education/SARCA/RAC-cadre-general-fp-tech.pdf

Moisan, M. (2020, June 2). Le téléphone de Mamadou sonne moins. *Le Soleil.* https://www.lesoleil.com/2020/06/02/le-telephone-de-mamadou-sonne-moins-289a4a18da64764813071d0dc57a0ff4?nor=true

Montminy, N. and Duval, S. (2022). Question de l'heure : Comment observer et soutenir les fonctions exécutives en contexte éducatif ? *La foucade*, 23(1), 15-17.

Mouillet, M.-C. et Barberet, D. (2005). *Le projet sans plume.* Éditions Qui plus est.

Moureaux, Frédérique. (n.d.). Les théories d'Edward T. Hall. www.uni-giessen.de/de/fbz/fb05/romanistik/sprx/frz/pers/moureaux/proj/seminar/g1g2-travail/G1-G2-3/g2-theories_Hall

Ordre des conseillers et conseillères d'orientation du Québec (OCCOQ). (2010). *Guide d'évaluation en orientation/Assessment Guide for Guidance for Career and Guidance Counselling.* https://www.orientation.qc.ca/medias/iw/Le-Guide-d-evaluation-en-orientation.pdf

Olry-Louis, I. (2020). Introduction au numéro thématique « Migrations internationales et orientation », *L'orientation scolaire et professionnelle* 49(3), 383-399 https://doi.org/10.4000/osp.12366

Oral History Association. (2009). Principles and Best Practices. www.oralhistory.org/about/principles-and-practices-revised-2009

Parkes, C.M. (1971). Psycho-social transitions: A field for study. *Social Science and Medicine, 5,* 101-115. doi.org/10.1016/0037-7856(71)90091-6

Parkes, C.M. (1975). Psycho-social Transitions: Comparison between Reactions to Loss of a Limb and Loss of a Spouse. *The British Journal of Psychiatry, 127,* 204-210. https://doi.org/10.1192/bjp.127.3.204

Pelletier, Benjamin. (2012, September 7). La communication indirecte – exemples, observations et réflexions. https://gestion-des-risques-interculturels.com/risques/la-communication-indirecte-exemples-observations-et-reflexions

Perdrix, S. (2013). *Efficacité du counseling d'orientation : impacts de l'alliance de travail et du contexte psychosocial.* Université de Lausanne.

Prévost, C. (2021). *Parcours d'apprentissage du français de réfugiés d'origine bhoutanaise dans la ville de Québec : Influences des mobilités, des apprentissages et des dynamiques familiales* [Thesis.] Université Laval.

Pocreau, J.-P. and Borges, L. M. (2006). Reconnaitre la difference: le défi de l'ethnopsychiatrie. Santé mentale au Québec, 31(2), 43-56. **https://doi.org/10.7202.014802ar**

Regroupement québécois des organismes pour le développement de l'employabilité (RQuODE). (2016). *Guide de référence pour les conseillers en développement de carrière intervenant auprès de la clientèle Inuit.* CERIC and the Kativik Regional Government. **https://ceric.ca/fr/publications/guide-de-reference-pour-les-conseillers-en-developpement-de-carriere-intervenant-aupres-de-la-clientele-inuit/**

Rey, L., Affodégon, W., Viens, I., Fathallah, H. and Arauz, M.J. (2019). La méthode photovoix. In V. Ridde and C. Dagenais (Eds.). *Évaluation des interventions de santé mondiale.* (pp. 83-123). Éditions science et bien commun and IRD Éditions.. **https://scienceetbiencommun.pressbooks.pub/evalsantemondiale/**

Richard, V. and Bombardier, A. (2020, December 9). *Parcours migratoire des demandeurs d'asile et des réfugiés : un outil d'évaluation et d'intervention incontournable* Webinar. Centre d'expertise sur le bien-être et l'état de santé physique des réfugiés et des demandeurs d'asile (CERDA). **https://cerda.info/parcours-pre-peri-post-migratoire-dune-personne-en-demande-dasile-vignette-clinique/**

Rive, J. and Roger, A. (2014). La communication interculturelle. In U. Mayrhofer (Ed.) *Les Grands auteurs en management international* (pp. 375-390). Éditions EMS.

Robert, V. (2021). *Le parcours tech des personnes réfugiées, du départ à la stabilité.* Techfugees. **https://techfugees.com/fr/all_news/le-parcours-tech-des-personnes-refugiees-du-depart-a-la-stabilite-retranscription-podcast-%F0%9F%8E%A7/**

Robertson, P. J. and Picard, F. (2021). An introduction to the special section on the Capability Approach to career guidance. *International Journal for Educational and Vocational Guidance, 21, 395–404.* **https://doi.org/10.1007/s10775-021-09462-7**

Roesti, C. (2019). *La transition professionnelle de personnes réfugiées. Le cas de bénéficiaire d'une structure d'accompagnement vers l'insertion professionnelle.* [Master's Dissertation.] Université de Neuchâtel. Dossiers de Psychologie et Éducation, 75.

Rousseau C. (2000). Les réfugiés à notre porte : violence organisée et souffrance sociale. Criminologie, 33(1), 185–201. **doi.org/10.7202/004743ar**

Rousseau, G. G. and Venter, D. J. L. (2009). Investigating the importance of factors related to career choice. *Management Dynamics,* 18(3), 2-14.

Sabatier, C. and Berry, J. (1994). Immigration et acculturation. In R.Y. Bourhis and J.-P. Leyens (Eds.), *Stéréotypes, discrimination et relation intergroupes* (pp. 261 291). Mardaga.

Salamanca, C. M. (2016). Agences de placement et de recrutement, travail immigrant et précarité à Montréal. In A.-M. D'Aoust and V.A. Reyes Bruneau (Eds.), Les Cahiers du CRIEC 39. *Immigration, diversité ethnoculturelle et citoyenneté* (pp.100-118). Université du Québec à Montréal.

Salhi, C., Scoglio, A.A.J., Ellis, H., Issa, O. and Lincoln, A. (2020). The relationship of pre- and post-resettlement violence exposure to mental health among refugees: a multi-site panel survey of Somalis in the US and Canada. *Social Psychiatry and Psychiatric Epidemiology, 56*, 1015-1023. https://doi.org/10.1007/s00127-020-02010-8

Savard, R., Michaud, G., Bilodeau, C. and Arseneau, S. (2007). L'effet de l'information sur le marché du travail dans le processus décisionnel relatif au choix de carrière. *Canadian Journal of Counselling and Psychotherapy, 41*(3). https://cjc-rcc.ucalgary.ca/article/view/58817

Schlossberg, N.K. (2005). Aider les consultants à faire face aux transitions : Le cas particulier des non-événements. *L'orientation Scolaire et Professionnelle, 34*(1), 85-101. doi.org/10.4000/osp.345

Schlossberg, N. K., Waters, E. B., and Goodman, J. (1995). *Counseling Adults in Transition: Linking Practice with Theory* (2nd Ed.). Springer Publishing Co.

Scoglio, A.A.J. and Salhi, C. (2021). Violence Exposure and Mental Health Among Resettled Refugees: A Systematic Review. *Trauma, Violence & Abuse, 22*(5), 1192-1208. Doi: 10.1177/1524838020915584

Sen, A. (2010). *L'idée de justice*. Flammarion.

Seufert, P. (1999). *Refugees as English Language Learners: Issues and Concerns*. Center for Applied Linguistics. www.cal.org/caela/esl_resources/digests/Refugee.html

Shanouda, F. and Yoshida, K. K. (2012). *Disability Oral History Toolkit*. The Centre for Independent Living in Toronto (CILT) and the Department of Physical Therapy at the University of Toronto. https://www.cilt.ca/cilt-resources/our-histories/

Statistique Canada. (2021). Série « Perspective géographique », Recensement de la population de 2021. www12.statcan.gc.ca/census-recensement/2021/as-sa/fogs-spg/page.cfm?topic=9&lang=F&dguid=2021A000011124

Sue, D. W. et Sue, D. (2015). *Counseling the Culturally Diverse: Theory and Practice*. Wiley.

Supeno, E., Chabot, J., Dionne, P. and Viviers, S. (2023). *Des compétences en advocacie sociale et profession-nelle propres à la pratique professionnelle des personnes conseillères d'orientation: composantes, attentes et avenue de réflexion* Conference Proceedings . L'Ordre des conseillers et conseillères d'orientation du Québec (OCCOQ).

Supeno, E.,Dionne, P., Viviers, S. and Rivard, L. (2020). L'advocacie sociale et professionnelle dans les professions en santé mentale et relations humaines : un tour d'horizon (1ère partie). *L'Orientation*, 10(1), 28-34.

Supeno, E. and Mongeau, V. (2015). Horizon informationnel sur la formation et le travail chez les jeunes adultes non diplômés en situation de précarité. *Nouveaux Cahiers de la Recherche en Éducation*, **18(1)**, **114-136.**

Udayar, S., Fedrigo, L., Durante, F., Clot-Siegrist, E. and Masdonati, J. (2020). Labour market integration of young refugees and asylum seekers: a look at perceived barriers and resources. *British Journal of Guidance & Counseling*, 49(2), 287-303.3. **https://doi.org/10.1080/03069885.2020.1858023**

Université de Sherbrooke. (n.d.) *Les Biais inconscients*. **https://www.usherbrooke.ca/edi/fileadmin/sites/edi/Feuillet_final.pdf.**

Van der Kolk, B. A. (2015). *The Body Keeps the Score: Brain, Mind, and Body in the Healing of Trauma*. Penguin.

Van Dijke, A., Hopman, J.A.B., and Ford, J.D. (2018). Affect dysregulation, psychoform dissociation, and adult relational fears mediate the relationship between childhood trauma and complex posttrau-matic stress disorder independent of the symptoms of borderline personality disorder. *European Journal of Psychotraumatology*, 9(1), **doi.org/10.1080/20008198.2017.1400878**

Vatz Laaroussi, M., Guilbert, L., Rachédi, L., Kanouté, F., Ansòn, L., Canales, T., León Correal, A., Presseau, A., Thiaw, M.-L. and Zivanovic Sarenac, J. (2012). De la transmission à la construction des savoirs et des pratiques dans les relations intergénérationnelles de femmes réfugiées au Québec. *Nouvelles pratiques sociales*, 25(1), 136–156. **https://doi.org/10.7202/1017387ar**

Vespia, K.M., Fitzpatrick, M.E., Fouad, N.A., Kantamneni, N. and Chen, Y.-L. (2010). Multicultural Career Counseling: A National Survey of Competencies and Practices. *The career development quarterly*, 59(sept. 2010), 54-71.

Vonnahme, L.A., Lankau, E.W., Ao, T., Shetty, S. and Cardozo, B.L. (2015). Factors Associated with Symptoms of Depression Among Bhutanese Refugees in the United States. *Journal of Immigrant Minority Health*, 17, 1705–1714. **https://doi.org/10.1007/s10903-014-0120-x**

Whiston, S.C., Rossier, J. and Hernandez Baron, P. M. (2016). The Working Alliance in Career Counseling: A Systematic Overview. *Journal of Career Assessment*, 24(4), 591-604. Doi: 10.1177/1069072715615849

Wilkinson, M. (2003). Undoing trauma: contemporary neuroscience. A Jungian clinical perspective. *Journal of Analytical Psychology, 48*(2), 235–253.
https://doi.org/10.1111/1465-5922.t01-1-00008

Zalaquett, C.P. and Chambers, L.A. (2017) Counseling Individuals Living in Poverty. *Journal of multicultural counseling and development, 45,* 152-161.
doi.org/10.1002/jmcd.12071

www.ingramcontent.com/pod-product-compliance
Lightning Source LLC
Chambersburg PA
CBHW042332030426
42335CB00027B/3315